A Voice
of Her Own

About the Author

Dr. Nancy Tischler is professor of English and Humanities and Director of Summer Session at the Pennsylvania State University in University Park, Pennsylvania. She has also taught at Susquehanna University, George Washington University, and the University of Arkansas. Dr. Tischler holds the B.Sc. in Education from Wilson Teachers College, Washington, D.C., in English and Art. She received her M.A. and Ph.D. (Phi Beta Kappa) in English literature from the University of Arkansas, having also participated as a Fulbright Scholar in the graduate studies program at the University College of the Southwest (University of London), England. She has done further postgraduate study at Harvard University in the Institute for Educational Management.

Dr. Tischler has been a Danforth Associate, editor-at-large for *Christianity Today,* and editor of *Susquehanna Studies,* and is a member of the executive committee of the Pennsylvania Humanities Council. She has served as a member of the board of advisors and as national president (two years) for the *Conference on Christianity and Literature* and on the advisory board for the *Tennessee Williams Newsletter.* She is listed in *Who's Who in Religion, Who's Who of American Women,* and *Contemporary Authors.* Her books include: *Tennessee Williams: Rebellious Puritan; Black Masks: Negro Characters in Modern Southern Fiction; Tennessee Williams* (Southern Writer's Series); *Legacy of Eve: Images of Women in the Bible;* and *Dorothy L. Sayers: A Pilgrim Soul.* She has authored dozens of scholarly articles and book reviews in more than fourteen journals and anthologies. This is her sixth book. She is married to attorney C. Merle Tischler and has two children, Eric and Grant.

A Voice
of Her Own

Women, Literature,
and Transformation

Nancy M. Tischler

ZONDERVAN PUBLISHING HOUSE
OF THE ZONDERVAN CORPORATION
GRAND RAPIDS. MICHIGAN 49506

PROBE MINISTRIES
INTERNATIONAL
DALLAS, TEXAS 75204

Copyright	© 1987 by Probe Ministries International
Library of Congress Cataloging in Publication Data	Tischler, Nancy Marie Patterson. A voice of her own. Bibliography: p. Includes index. 1. American literature—Women authors— History and criticism. 2. English literature— Women authors—History and criticism. 3. Women and literature. 4. Christianity and literature. I. Title. PS147.T57 1987 810'.9'9287 86–26740
ISBN	0–310–33951–0

Place of Printing	*Printed in the United States of America*
Series Editor	Steven W. Webb, Probe Ministries
Assistant Editor	Carol Crawford
Design	Inside cover design by Paul Lewis Book design by Louise Bauer

87 88 89 90 91 / CH / 7 6 5 4 3 2 1

What Is Probe?

Probe Ministries is a nonprofit corporation organized to provide perspective on the integration of the academic disciplines and historic Christianity. The members and associates of the Probe team are actively engaged in research as well as lecturing and interacting in thousands of university classrooms throughout the United States and Canada on topics and issues vital to the university student.

Christian Free University books should be ordered from Zondervan Publishing House (in the United Kingdom from the Paternoster Press), but further information about Probe's materials and ministries may be obtained by writing to Probe Ministries International, P.O. Box 801046, Dallas, Texas 75204.

74972

Contents

Foreword

When any author chooses to write on a touchy, indeed explosive, subject such as this analysis of women's studies and women's literature, she must be prepared for a variety of responses to her work. On these pages Dr. Nancy Tischler stands in the midst of a battle raging in Western culture over the changing role of women and the reactions of two potentially hostile audiences—supporters, of various persuasions, of the women's movement on one side and the Evangelical church, of which she is a part, on the other.

This polarization between "Christians" and "feminists" is an unfortunate one, as if the two groups could be evenly divided into two well-defined lumps: the "good guys" and "bad guys." Such a stance presumptuously assumes that orthodox Evangelicals care nothing for a woman's rights and needs, and anyone who does care automatically has joined philosophical hands with Gloria Steinem and Bella Abzug.

With this issue we are faced, not with two poles, but rather with *two continua*. The thinking represented in the women's movement ranges all the way from the radical who, with real hostility and resentment, is out to compete with and displace all male dominion, to the homemaker who demands her cherished right and dignity to be exactly that and nothing more. Christians span the extremes of ignoring or trying to explain away genuine biblical constraints to the use of the Bible as a baptizer of those cultural patterns with which they feel most comfortable. What then is the true Christian position? Simply this: We are *for* the genuine biblical constraints and we are *for* women. We desire that they be all God meant them to be as sisters in the body of Christ. And a woman's calling may or may not include marriage and childbearing. It may or may not include vocational and educational interests. And women have this freedom in Christ and in both Testaments, even if some would seek to deny them such. What a woman does with her life flows from her individual gifts, needs, and priorities. These vary as widely among women as they do among men. True Christian liberty for the woman, like the man, is the freedom in Christ to balance her gifts, needs, and priorities so that they are maximized in the context of the choices she has made for her life. We must not compare or compete; such is not the biblical way.

Christians in particular need to read this book. I needed to read it. In fact, I confess no small amount of growth in doing so. In places I was strongly uncomfortable, and I had to honestly face the reasons why. Part of my struggle came from the author's discussion of some of the thinking found in the women's movement in *positive* terms. This was a new experience for me. Could any of this "new wine," as Dr. Tischler calls it, possibly be good? Yes. Some of it is. After reading the book, I can say with genuine conviction that I am *for* the phenomenon of the women's movement to the extent that it frees Christian women from cultural (not biblical) constraints that have discouraged or thwarted them in their attempts to experience in their personal lives the maximum freedom they have in Christ. A Christian man assumes at the outset that he has this freedom. Most Christian women do not, and they fear expressing it would identify them with "the enemy."

Dr. Tischler has written with insight and courage. Her analysis is sound and scholarly, not polemical nor emotional. She reviews the real struggles women have faced through the centuries in their efforts to attain personal fulfillment and true equality. Her approach is neither hostile nor judgmental. Rather, she *describes* the feelings, frustrations, and needs of women who have sought to express their God-given creativity and gifts in a world largely dominated by men. She comments on this phenomenon among both Christian and non-Christian writers. The reader is thus cautioned not to make the fatal mistake of reading into her text "prescription" where only "description" is intended.

In these pages there is no quarrel with biblical constraints nor with male leadership responsibilities in home and church. There is also here no crusade to revise Scripture for the inclusion of feminine appellations to the Deity. What *is* challenged are the traditional assumptions—even among many sincere Christians—for defining what women in general and Christian women in particular can and cannot do.

Much of what Dr. Tischler has to say focuses on the cultural prisons from which women are increasingly emerging and how they have attained new-found and unprecedented opportunity for creative expression. The challenge for the Christian reader thus becomes one of sorting out the kernels from the husks and being able to genuinely applaud those elements of the women's movement that are removing cultural wineskins and restoring a true, biblical freedom to women.

The discerning reader will come away from this book with fresh insight about the depth, width, and breadth of opportunity God has provided for all His creatures—both male and female. An additional value will be the instructive exercise of looking over the shoulder of a fine Christian scholar who has chosen not to remain aloof from, but stand in the midst of, those female voices—past and present—crying out for personal fulfillment.

Ultimately Christians recognize that this fulfillment can be realized only in the nurture of a personal relationship with Christ. And it is our Lord Himself who gives true dignity and meaning to all personal choices of men and women alike. When we become aware of this, we discover that the "new wine" being freshly tasted by some in this book is really as old as the Evangel itself.

Jimmy Williams, President
Probe Ministries International

Preface

Explosive new ideas often threaten to burst the seams of old social forms—like new wine, they call for new skins with greater elasticity. Modern literature by and about women is also a new vintage, also explosive, also demanding new forms.

This book is my effort to provide a sense of the flavor of this wine, to describe its fresh qualities, and to consider appropriate skins that might contain it without constraining it. The study is only *a* Christian perspective; other Christians may come to other conclusions by equally valid paths.

I approach women's studies as a woman, comfortable with the Protestant, Evangelical, and Reformed traditions. I am a middle-class college professor who loves literature, an American from a small town in central Pennsylvania, happily married for more than a quarter of a century to a man who is sensitive to women, and the mother of two sons and no daughters. I believe that the Christian family is one of God's richest—and most complex—blessings. Other writers whom I have studied have very different perspectives because they stand alone or beside very different mates at very different vantage points. We share some ideas and differ on others.

The term *women's literature* also needs some explanation. Not all writing has great aesthetic value and would not therefore fit into the category properly called *literature*. I do include a number of works of psychology, philosophy, and social and religious criticism in this study, but they are not the literature that I consider central. The short stories, poems, novels, and plays discussed in this book may be by women or about women or both. Some of the most important authors involved are men who have displayed that quality so admired in Keats's poetry—

"negative capability." This is the ability to project oneself into another creature's skin and feel what he or she is feeling, to see the world from a fresh point of view.

I have also focused the discussion on a selection of recent literature in English. Culture and language are enormously important forces in literary production. Hebraic and Hellenic literature are the foundations for modern thought and certainly must be cited in the discussion. But the modern woman living in England or America, speaking English, has very different problems and opportunities and means of expression than these women of ancient and alien cultures.

Modern literature has hundreds of authors I could have cited, many of them as good as those I arbitrarily chose. The field has an embarrassment of riches that form the source of frustration for me as a scholar who prefers to be thorough, and a delight for me as a woman and a critic who applauds the liberating spirit that has allowed so many lights to shine forth into our world.

Book Abstract

Against the backdrop of the modern women's movement, the author shows us how women have overcome a variety of obstacles in history to demonstrate the same quality of creativity in artistic and social endeavor as their male counterparts.

Dr. Tischler describes the characterizations of women portrayed in writings over the years and the literary forms women favored when they at last began to write for public audiences. She points out the revolution in values in the arts that could be brought about by the influence of the feminine viewpoint. And she offers guidelines for readers, encouraging a thoughtful and discerning sampling of the new works by and about women.

Along the way, she asks and attempts to give cautious answers to some of the most difficult questions that fair-minded, justice-seeking people—both Christian and non-Christian—ask. For example, why are there so few notable women writers in literary history, gathered in such a few years and few places in the world? How is this lack of female authorship related to women's historical exclusion from public life? To religious tradition and church history? To the demands of family life? Dr. Tischler explores these questions and invites us to examine the relationship between women and literature. As the reader discovers these relationships, the impact of the women's movement, its values, its foibles, its merits, and its problems become increasingly clear.

Finally, Dr. Tischler calls for grace and sensitivity in handling women's place in the creative arts and the larger cultural sphere. Her perspective demonstrates clear thinking and demands an unemotional and balanced response from three crucial arenas: the feminist movement itself; the church; and, of course, the individual reader of women's literature.

chapter one

Escape From the Velvet Cage

The author describes the history of women's exclusion from the literary world and the gradual opening of that world to women as the women's movement has created change. She describes our cultural grounding in Scripture and urges audiences to read with discrimination.

"Thank God I was not born a woman." So goes the ancient Jewish male morning prayer. "Excluded, excluded, excluded," is the way author Tillie Olsen sums up woman's lot—"excluded from council, ritual, activity, language, when there was neither biological nor economic reason to be excluded."[1]

But what difference does this make? Writing, after all, is a private business. The reader may ask, why does it matter that a woman has been excluded? Let her write of her exclusion from her exclusion. If the author is any good, surely she can break out of social categories and transcend sexual stereotypings.

Behind the Lace Curtain

A few examples can help us to understand the price such a person must pay. Take, for instance, an early modern novelist, Ellen Glasgow.[2]

The experience of this determined southerner can help others understand the difficulties that lurked in the path of the female writer in turn-of-the-century America.

Everything seemed to conspire to prevent her success. Glasgow was a part of the sheltered upper-middle-class womanhood, cherished for her ornamental qualities. When Ellen was a child, her mother restricted her lunches to the flaky beaten biscuits and white meat of chicken appropriate for a lady. One day a young hooligan at school stole her lunch. This prank proved a catastrophe for the child. Her mother immediately removed little Ellen from school and thereby ended forever her formal education. Maternal protection and class privilege became her golden cage.

She was hungry for knowledge but thwarted at every turn. A southern woman (like a southern black—though for different reasons) was not allowed to use the public library. Fortunately Glasgow had a family mentor who understood her "unfeminine" love of books. With the help of her thoughtful brother-in-law, she did buy, beg, and borrow enough books to provide for herself a rich (though uneven) education.

While still in her teens, she wrote her first novel. But again she needed her brother-in-law's help. A lady would have no access to the means of publication. He sent the book off for her to a friend, Price Collier, who was a prominent New York publisher. Knowing nothing about the publishing business, she naïvely expected an answer within a week. Not hearing by then, she packed her bags and went to New York to find out why Mr. Collier was so slow in responding. He graciously offered to take the lovely young southerner out for an elegant lunch. Over their leisurely meal, he admitted that he had not read her book and did not plan to do so. In a kindly paternal gesture, he counseled the charming young woman to "stop writing and go back South and have some babies."

Glasgow never forgot her anger, pain, humiliation, and newfound determination. Nor did she allow Mr. Collier to go unscathed into eternity. She chronicled the experience in her autobiography, *The Woman Within*. She never married, and she never had babies. But she did take his advice and go back South. In her long life she wrote numerous best sellers, many of which have become classics. (My favorites are *Barren Ground* and *Vein of Iron*.) Glasgow is the rare case of a woman tough enough to break out of her cage.

Her experience, though more dramatic than most, was typical of the policy of polite exclusion so common at the beginning of the twentieth century. Although more conservative than much of the rest of America, Ellen Glasgow's Richmond was not unique. Her family treated young women like fragile flowers, her community kept them ignorant and untarnished and supposedly satisfied with their ornamental role. And she was forced to rely on an understanding male friend. These are the patterns we find over and over in middle-class and upper-class female lives. The lower classes, on the other hand, were freer to work, to explore, to be independent. But they were generally so exploited and exhausted that they had little appetite for writing or reading books. Theirs was an economic and educational cage far more cruel and demeaning than hers.

Stories like Theodore Dreiser's *Sister Carrie* (1900) or Thomas Hardy's *Tess of the d'Urbervilles* (1891) provide some glimpses of the work available to lower-class women at the turn of the century. Social historians tell of the mills and factories in even more graphic detail. Literature rarely flourishes in such a marginal existence. Writing requires leisure and privacy—a "room of one's own."

This is equally true for the male artist. Until quite recently the lower- and even middle-class men were excluded from the art world, both by education and opportunity. A struggling artist needed a patron in order to support himself and his work, and such a patron could be demanding and limiting. With the eighteenth century came the accessibility of education and the decreasing costs of print, thus making it possible for an author to earn a living by writing. The public proved as demanding an audience as the earlier patrons, but at least authors of the middle class and even the lower class had a better chance to use their talents to earn their livelihood. This democratization of art was eventually to open a door for women to enter the literary profession.[3]

The lace curtains that restricted woman to her "proper sphere" were not peculiar to America. In England at about the same time, Dorothy L. Sayers found herself thwarted in parallel but not identical ways.[4] Born in Oxford, she was tutored by her scholarly father, who was himself a rebel against the Oxford tradition of male scholars and female helpmeets. No pretty southern belle, this adventuresome tomboy was encouraged from her youth to read widely and to study and to compete for academic prizes. Yet when she won her scholarship to Somerville, one of the first of the Oxford colleges for women, she found the life there claustrophobic and frustrating. Chaperones attended the young ladies as they went to their classes, and many of the male professors simply ignored their female students. They addressed their lectures pointedly and exclusively to the men. Nonetheless, Sayers persevered because she loved the studies. Eventually she sat for her exams, which women had only been recently admitted to take with Oxford men. To her delight, she earned a "first," the highest grade possible—a real prize. But she was not allowed to graduate that year. Women did not receive Oxford degrees until ten years later—1925.

After leaving Oxford, she was not showered with job offers. Instead, like most women until recently, she found she could teach in a girls' school. The only means to economic success for most women has been by way of a man—through inheritance or marriage. Dorothy Sayers, the conspicuously plain daughter of a poor clergyman, had little chance for either path. Yet she believed that money represented freedom—the freedom to study and to write. Excluded from those male-dominated careers that might allow her economic success, she turned to writing mystery stories. Her series about the effete detective Lord Peter was an astonishing financial success. Her creation, Lord Peter Wimsey, proved to be the male who allowed her to break free, to write plays and essays and translations.[5]

Only a fiercely determined spirit could break out of the mummy wrappings of English social life to become such an articulate and independent voice. Her translations of Dante and of the *Song of Roland* were the most widely read in the history of those works.[6] But the snobbish male scholars of Oxford and Cambridge never included her in their ranks. Women, even when grudgingly recognized for their genius, have regularly been excluded from the community of scholars.

Opening the Window

Even after Oxford cautiously and reluctantly opened its doors and its degrees to women, the university resisted opening up its library to them. Apparently Englishmen, like Americans, thought that women could not be trusted with books. In *A Room of One's Own* Virginia Woolf noted that though she was invited to speak at "Oxbridge," she was not allowed to use the library without a male companion.[7]

As a result of this insult, she walked away and mulled over the problems of such exclusion. Wondering why no woman ever wrote Shakespeare's plays, she started imagining the kind of life that a sister of Shakespeare would have had. The result was a seminal book in women's studies, *A Room of One's Own*. In it she describes Shakespeare's fictitious sister, her exclusion from education, from experience, from craft, from encouragement or opportunity. Judith Shakespeare ends in suicide. The narrative concludes with these powerful words: ". . . any woman born with a great gift in the sixteenth century would certainly have gone crazed, shot herself, or ended her days in some lonely cottage outside the village, half witch, half wizard, feared and mocked at."[8]

It has now been more than fifty years since Virginia Woolf wrote these words. Unfortunately she committed suicide when she sensed the approach of World War II, but the frustration and exclusion that so rankle the creative woman are still very much alive. Her own books continue to be an inspiration for new generations of students, many of whom have come to agree with her arguments and appreciate her novels and essays. Few people have done more to advance the cause of women's literature than Virginia Woolf.

Our century has seen door after door opened to women—education, public institutions, careers, and libraries. Many of the barriers that hedged them about were so ancient and venerable as to seem inevitable and impenetrable. The changes in human life because of these breached barriers—especially in England and America—have been less like those wrought by a revolution than those caused by an earthquake. The whole redefinition of the role of women and the consequent reorganization of society have shaken our culture to its very foundations.

A Voice of Her Own

Scholars in a variety of fields—economics, education, history, law, philosophy, and sociology—have turned their focus to this modern phenomenon. In any listing of recent scholarly and popular works, the group of women's books is impressive. In the last decade, largely because of the efforts of a sizeable band of bright and determined scholars, women's studies courses had proliferated nationwide to an estimated twenty thousand by 1981. *The New York Times* noted, "Since its inception a decade ago, women's studies has developed from a smattering of courses regarded by some academics as trivial or unduly political into a burgeoning new discipline that has been firmly established in both training and research." Just as black scholars have produced a whole body of serious scholarship, so feminist scholars have reexamined the male-oriented history, language, literature, religion, sociology, psychology, medicine, etc., from this new perspective. Unfortunately, women's studies courses have tended to attract primarily women, preaching to "the committed." At the same time, they have encouraged like-minded women to form a network that encourages and supports members of that community.

And now feminist scholars are becoming more included, serving as officers in national scholarly organizations and increasingly entering into the mainstream of academic life. This will probably result in gradually including some of women's perceptions in all college courses rather than in having separate courses for the study of women's issues.

The View From the Room

The impact of women's studies is more important than the number of courses can suggest. Once all of us have had our consciousness raised, some ideas will always afterwards seem suspect, some phrases will always seem condescending. We all know that the language is now changing to accommodate women. *Man* and *he* as inclusive terms that refer to both men and women is passing out of usage. We all think more carefully about our choice of words, stumbling over *chairman* when we remember that the man in the case may be a woman. The resultant clumsiness suggests that we are in the midst of a language transition of some comprehensiveness.

20

But more than the words, the ideas and attitudes will never again be quite the same. Things have changed so rapidly that even as recent an author as Ernest Hemingway may never again seem quite so noble to us. Once we have thought about his stereotypical view of women, his acquiescent beauty who ministers to the macho male seems merely a figment of the adolescent male imagination.

Homer, on the other hand, looks even more impressive as we consider the realistic sketches of Helen and Andromache he included in the *Iliad* some millennia back. In fact, one of the measures of our growth in knowledge and sensitivity is the increased number of people who now read Virginia Woolf and Dorothy L. Sayers and Ellen Glasgow, and who sympathize with their concerns. These same readers would now encourage bright young girls to stay in school, to take books out of the library, and perhaps even to try writing novels.

Knowledge is, after all, a living thing. It grows and changes. Some parts wither away while others blossom. The frontiers of knowledge keep shifting. One day's wilderness becomes the next day's settlement. And the settlement can in turn flourish and then deteriorate into a slum that will eventually need to be renovated or abandoned. The great Puritan poet John Milton put it more eloquently in the *Areopagitica*. He said that knowledge is like the body of Osiris. When the god died, his parts were widely scattered. The god's beloved sister sought to reconstruct the mutilated body of her brother by searching out those scattered remnants, but the whole was never again quite complete. Truth is like this for us. We seek to reconstruct it, but we never will see it whole until at death we see "face to face."

One would think that in an area as old as the study of women there is little more to learn. Certainly all of the pieces should have long since been collected and fitted into the puzzle where they belong. But the new study of women has uncovered an enormous hitherto neglected body of knowledge, albeit represented by just as enormous a variety of interpretive viewpoints. It may turn out that we have only half of the puzzle and are looking at that upside down. Our understanding of history has focused almost exclusively on the activities of men and neglected the activities of women. The English language itself is skewed to describe the exaggerated importance of the male. What we now

A Voice of Her Own

need to do is to match this received knowledge with the vast and scattered bits of the unorthodox knowledge to try to piece together the body of truth.

Because it would be impossible in such a brief work as this to survey all the issues that emerge from this burgeoning body of knowledge and to trace the historical roots of the women's movement itself, I have limited this study to one of the major areas of women's studies—literature. At the same time, I can provide a glimpse of the other fields and point to some interesting movements and concerns. But I must acknowledge that literature itself is a vast field, too vast to be covered in such a slender study. As I noted earlier, I have chosen to focus on the Western cultures and especially those that are English-speaking in order to discuss familiar habits of thought. Although most of my examples are recent, some of the comments would hold true for women in many cultures and in many ages. Nor have I found it possible to restrict the discussions to women writers; too many men have written fine, sensitive works that characterize and explain much about women. I have also found it impossible to speak of modern English and American literature without reference to their classical and biblical roots.

Through the Glass Darkly—and Then . . .

To some extent Scripture itself is (among other things) literature. Biblical poetry and narrative are the deliberate and artistic arrangement of words and ideas to present characters and events and theology for readers and hearers of the words. Scripture is not fiction in the sense of being stories made up by human authors. Nonetheless, it may include fiction (parables, dreams, etc.). It describes historical personages and events in such a way as to order our thinking and to help us to understand the truth. And it is the world's most impressive mine for the creative arts.

Even most of those modern authors who supposedly scorn Scripture and consider themselves thoroughly pagan have been raised in a civilization largely formed by Scripture. The images of women, the concept of history, the values that we share are traceable—in most cases—to the Bible and to the Judeo-Christian culture. No serious study of literature can ignore this incalculable debt. Even so-called secular literature resonates with scriptural echoes.

Thus we speak of Eve and the role of woman as temptress. Or we think of the rarity of Deborah—the woman as political and national leader. Or we admire Ruth for her submissive love. And we hate Jezebel for her trickery. Our attitudes and our terminology have clearly been formed by such powerful images. If we decide to judge Lilith (the mythological child-stealing witch of Babylonian folklore) as a heroine, Bathsheba as a victim, or Esther as a con artist, we are deliberately bringing modern attitudes to bear on ancient people. The subsequent judgments may therefore be both perverse and inappropriate. But even a perverse use of Scripture still presumes some knowledge of it: we can only reverse or distort that which we know, albeit dimly in the first place. The fun-house mirror reminds us of the beauty of the original creature that it distorts.

When we Christians are puzzled or disturbed by changes in our world, we seek to remind ourselves of our grounding in Scripture. When we see women relegated to the kitchen, we recall the voice of Christ reminding Martha that Mary had found the better way. When we see a woman storm her way to the top of the corporate world, we recall His voice reminding us that the first shall be last. When women are treated as only instruments of pleasure, we remember Christ's clear recognition of each man's and woman's individual value for his or her total being. Christian readers, by such echoes as this, use Scripture as the touchstone for judging life and literature. This rock on which our lives are built can hold against all the storms of contemporary theory and false religion.

Scriptural literature provides us words to live by. But other more popular and evanescent words (the Book of the Month, or the Idea of the Moment) also affect us. We may not deliberately look to them for spiritual guidance, but they do nonetheless shape our lives. No concerned parent, no responsible Christian can ignore the importance of the reading eye and the receptive mind, for even the discerning mind may be unduly, or perhaps unwittingly, influenced.

My mother used to say to me, "You are what you eat." Now I say to my sons (with every bit as little impact), "You are what you watch and what you read." TV and films and books help fix our values. We consider one woman to be beautiful and another vulgar; one sexual code honorable and another depraved—all in large part because of what we read. The arts have influenced many value changes in modern life. The increasing acceptance of pornography, of obscene and profane language, of "trial" marriages, of divorce as "liberation," of homosexuality as a "normal" sexual preference, of abortion as "choice"—these are all values entering our lives in large part through the arts.

Reading, then, is serious business. It can twist our lives and thoughts. It can also strengthen our values and enlarge our understanding. For Christians, a handy yardstick is always available in the words and example of Christ. Even though we find painfully few talented Christian artists among the recognized modern greats, we have the voice of this Eternal Critic always in our hearts to help us judge and appreciate the worldly artists. With the guidance of the Holy Spirit, Christians can read widely and discriminate clearly; with His help we can try to reassemble the broken body of Truth.

Biblical truth is not itself simple. The statements that range from Genesis to Revelation about women are varied and often difficult to reconcile. A single author—such as Paul—may say at one point that women should be subject to their husbands and at another that there is neither male nor female in Christ. This *apparently* contradictory nature of scriptural messages creates a lively tension for us, keeping our interpretations from becoming simplistic and final. Ours is a faith for searchers and growers, capable of balancing off ideas and values in a creative manner. We know that Christ spoke of the family with both love and scorn, that He saw individualism as sometimes good and sometimes bad. He loves to hand us puzzles that force us to find answers for ourselves. As Paul noted, Christians can start with being spoon-fed on pabulum, but in time they have to mature and test their teeth on "strong meat."

Our ideas about women are full of unresolved conflicts, often, in fact, conflicts between "goods." Analyzing, testing, and evaluating these ideas is tough work for mature Christians, those not afraid to leave the nursery of pat answers and undertake the perilous journey into ambiguities toward mature understanding.

Christian liberty comes when we have in us the mind of Christ, so that we see all things through His eyes. We are free to read most anything because we know how to judge its worth. After we decide that an artist is talented, that her book is original, then we should consider whether we can accept the implied attitudes and underlying philosophy of her fictional world. Having so great a Guide, we are potentially more discriminating critics than those who follow every will-o'-the-wisp.

chapter two

Woman as Hero in Her Story

The author describes the growth of women's literature as it moves through five stages toward maturity: reporting, self-examination, copying, breaking away, and the authentic voice.

Before we look at the artist and the work she has created, we must understand something of the process of art. Like people, literature goes through a series of stages to arrive at its most mature phase. Certainly with such an enormous change as that created by the women's movement, the altering of author, subject, and form in literature must be a process rather than an event. The woman as author will generally await the moment in history that is right for her. Most of us need the ideas, the forms, the training in the craft, the encouragement, the audience, and the opportunity before we become creators. Art does not just erupt; it grows and changes and finds its best form.

By its very nature, art is ordered and selective. The real world that it reflects is not. The story that we choose to tell is not a simple mirror of events or people. It is selected bits of reality, recombined with fiction to build a new reality. Any thoughtful writer in touch with the world around her knows that the story she is telling is not exact truth. It is only a quick glimpse of a corner of one person's perception of the truth. No one can, in fact, do what each of us promises to do in court: to tell the truth, the whole truth, and nothing but the truth. We do not even know what we do not know—that is, we do not know what has limited our perception.

It is the very transience of our world that makes fiction in some ways so satisfying. While we are faced with the rush of time and events, the character in the story stands outside of time. This creation, this unchanging fiction, is in some ways more true than the transitory facts themselves. No wonder the Greek philosopher Aristotle preferred poetry to history; poetry is more universal than history. The facts of the historical events are occurrences of the moment that then vanish. The truth of the poem is more permanent; it applies to other ages and to other cultures.

Many of the books we now read about women are heavily factual. They are full of detail about poets' lives. They chronicle the intricate relationships between great men and their mothers and daughters and mistresses and wives. They catalogue the everyday activities of women at various periods in history. All of this is an effort to open traditional male-oriented history to tell the long-lost story of women's lives through the ages. This process of fact finding is obviously the first crucial step in understanding the undocumented half of the human race and of human history. Without some basis in fact, we can only cry out lamely against stereotypes and half-truths. Although this process of scholarly investigation is not art, it can form the basis for art.

A people moving from primitive art forms to mature ones generally goes through a series of stages. (American literary critic Robert Spiller speaks of these in his classic study, *The Cycle of American Literature,* which I am adapting for the purposes of this study.)[9]

The Reporting Stage

The first stage is reporting. In American history this stage includes the letters and journals that chronicle life in an alien situation. In women's studies these are the lonely journals that have revealed what it was like to be a woman on a Georgia plantation in the early nineteenth century or to live through the Civil War, not as a warrior, but as a woman.

Fanny Kemble, for example, was a famous British actress in the nineteenth century. She married a wealthy young man from Philadelphia whose wealth came primarily from slave labor. When she went with him to live on his Georgia plantation, she saw slavery in all its horror. The shock of the experience led her to write a detailed diary. This journal has proven a rich source for studies in the culture of slavery. It took the alien eye and sensitive ear of Fanny Kemble to chronicle the habits of dance and song, the speech among the slaves.[10]

Mary Chestnutt, on the other hand, was no stranger to the South. She knew it thoroughly from the inside as the wife of a prominent politician. Her *Diary from Dixie* is the detailed chronicle of the Civil War told from the woman's point of view.[11] She sees less of the glory and the brilliantly planned maneuvers and more of the human suffering. Such authors give us the other side of events, the private view of the family members who have to deal with the aftereffects of the great public events—those that have to mop up and stitch up history's messes.

In the reporting stage, we also have the modern letter writers who show their own private worlds. Recent publications of letters have revealed much about Virginia Woolf: her wit, her frank and pointed commentary, and her passionate friendships with both men and women, as well as fascinating details of her private life. She was a part of the brilliant Bloomsbury Group—a collection of talented and prestigious art critics and writers from a variety of disciplines who gathered in the Bloomsbury section of London in the 1920s. The letters to and about members of the group underline their love of conversation and of the arts, as well as their unconventional behavior.

Another set of letters from the same period and the same city reveals a completely different style of life and thought. Dorothy L. Sayers shows herself in her letters, as in her other writings, to be passionately involved with ideas and conversation. Although she sought to be a private person, who became public only in speeches or writing, her letters reveal her love affairs, her tragic marriage to an alcoholic ne'er-do-well, the birth of her illegitimate child, and her courageous life. Only a few of the letters have been published so far, but they are tantalizing evidence of a great body of lively information about a complex and gifted woman.

Letters by authors like Virginia Woolf or Dorothy L. Sayers tell us a great deal of the experience of women facing the pressures of early twentieth-century life. They also demonstrate the difference between the lives lived by those who have an enduring faith in God and those whose faith is fixed in human creativity or human reason alone. A war can arouse a Sayers to new heights of service and faith, while it can drive a Woolf to despair and suicide.

Other writers, with more of an eye to publication, have told us more selectively about the experiences of their lives. Pioneers in their work, they have left us autobiographies to explain the rocky path that the woman who seeks to write seriously has had to take.

Each of these women is very different from each of the others. Ellen Glasgow's *The Woman Within* tells of her loneliness, her appetite for literature, her friendships. It is the touching chronicle of growing up in Richmond in the early days of the century, modified by her pride in the work she accomplished.

Lillian Hellman, on the other hand, in *An Unfinished Woman, Pentimento,* and other essays, tells of her far more urbane life.[12] Dividing her years between New Orleans and New York, sharing that life with a southern Gentile mother and a European Jewish father, Hellman grew strong and alert. She went to college in New York, found jobs in publishing, lived an unorthodox life filled with love affairs, an abortion, travel abroad, and finally a long liaison with Dashiell Hammett, author of *The Maltese Falcon* and other popular works of detective fiction. Through him she was drawn into meetings with Communists and into confrontations with the House Committee on Un-American Activities. Her story is full of anecdotes about famous people in New York and Hollywood and Washington, of love for the now-deceased Hammett, and of anger at then-Congressman Richard Nixon and anticommunist Joseph McCarthy. As a member of the black-listed Hollywood writers, she lost her means of livelihood and her house, recovering economically only in her final years. In time she became again a best-selling author, but rarely for her plays. Memoirs (such as the recently filmed *Julia,* a fictionalized account of her anti-Nazi activities) created a new Hellman revival just before her death.

A third such pioneering figure is Maya Angelou. She represents an even more extraordinary career. From a childhood in the black section of a small Arkansas town, this amazing woman was to rise to international prominence. Starting with *I Know Why the Caged Bird Sings*, she has chronicled her love affairs, her artistic growth, her political involvements, and her changing sense of self.[13]

Such works, though by no means models for Christian faith or action, are invaluable for the facts and feelings that they lay bare and for occasional flashes of elegant expression or passion. They open up our understanding to other lives and allow us to extend our sympathies as we share those experiences.

The Image-in-the-Mirror Stage

In Spiller's pattern this informative early reporting period is followed by a phase of self-examination—that is, the image-in-the-mirror stage. In women's studies examples of phase two have been particularly colorful. The French existentialist Simone de Beauvoir's *Second Sex*, for example, is a work rich in philosophic and psychological explanations of the role of woman in life and in art.[14] This work, spanning the centuries, analyzes woman's role in many cultures. The author knows an enormous body of European literature and art from which she draws freely to explain overarching patterns. She can point, for instance, to the masculine patterns of transcendence and the feminine patterns of immanence. Thus one expects the hero to go out on his grand adventures while the woman hovers at the hearth awaiting his return. Her comfort is that, while missing his adventures, she also misses his perils—and therefore outlives him. Few books are as important to women's studies as is this masterpiece.

Also important in this second stage, but for other reasons, is a book like modern feminist Betty Friedan's *Feminine Mystique*, which incited masses of bored housewives to near riot in the late sixties.[15] Her angry blast at the role of woman in postwar American culture gave voice to the wrath of many other frustrated housewives. It inspired such films as *Diary of a Mad Housewife*. It encouraged thousands of women to reenter colleges and the job market, and drew strident responses from

31

men and women alike. Defenders of the traditional homemaker united on the side of the famous counterattack, *The Total Woman*, by Evangelical writer Marabelle Morgan.[16] Right or wrong, Friedan called into question the value of staying at home, producing and rearing children. The consequent reevaluation of roles and relationships left many traditional women feeling confused and neglected. More recently, Friedan has returned to acknowledge the value of romance and family. Even radical British feminist Germaine Greer now admits that women find enormous joy in bearing and rearing children. Time and nature have tempered these zealots.[17]

Other books are more literary than social texts. Virginia Woolf's classic, *A Room of One's Own*, combines passion with vast knowledge of history and literature, joining gracefully individual experience and research. As noted earlier, her fanciful imagination plays with the question of why women did not write Shakespeare's plays. Her response is dazzling. By creating the fictional character of Shakespeare's sister Judith, Woolf poignantly demonstrates why women have so rarely written great art. Other books of hers deal with individual authors and events. Especially effective are the essays of *The Common Reader* series,[18] which provide some of the best and earliest feminist critiques of literature. She interprets Victorian poet Christina Rossetti and others with a touching awareness of their caged existence and their lyric purity.[19]

Other studies, like *Sexual Politics* by modern feminist Kate Millett, are more bookish and polemic, smacking of the scholar's study.[20] The rash of such studies in the past quarter century testifies to the number of women in academia at the time that the women's movement got under way. It also demonstrates the talent of the creative imagination and the level of concern among readers. The ever-growing host of books by and about women that combine experience with scholarship have frequently proven both exciting and valuable. The liberated imagination can be a delight. But liberation and novelty can also be a trap. The latest popular idea can captivate even the brightest scholars, luring them away from enduring truth.

The expanding bibliography of women's studies signals a solid market for women's literature and consequent access to the publishers. While the rhetoric is modulating, the sensitivity seems to be escalating. Female writers, having vented their pent-up frustration, can now shift to a third phase of development.

The Copycat Stage

Spiller notes that a people usually copy before they innovate. Rather than risk originality or an expression of fresh experience in fresh forms, artists tend to imitate the popular forms of the dominant culture. Thus Americans (men and women) were inclined to make wooden copies of British poetry and novels before they wrote of indigenous experience. As we know, art usually grows out of art, not out of life. We know how to draw because we see another person drawing. We know how to express an idea because we have heard another person express a similar idea. We alter very little of the given forms as we inch along in human progress.

For such new fields as black studies or women's studies, this propensity to emulate is particularly ironic. It forces the creative artist into copying the shape of the very ideas that he or she rejects. The black hero may seem nothing more than a white man in a black face. The female hero may be little more than a man in a woman's clothing. The essence is not altered.

If the male hero in the older novel or short story followed the usual patterns, he took either the romantic path (bound outward into adventure) or the classic path (returning to home and death). In either case, the image is one of the voyage or the journey. Yet many women never make the "voyage out" in any physical sense. Woman has been identified with the home and rarely goes more than a short distance from it. How can the adventure story in its traditional form be the right skin for the new wine of woman's experience?

In most novels the hero is the person who acts, the subject who performs the actions that form the plot. But traditionally the woman has been passive, the object in such stories, the person acted for or upon. Thus women are the objects or accessories in most of the older stories: the reason for the battle of Troy, the goal for the journey back to Ithaca, the prize for the invader of the Labyrinth. They are not co-workers participating actively in those battles or adventures. The rare woman in the Shakespearean plays or the medieval romances who did join in the action usually disguised herself, dressing up like a man, relaxing into her femininity only for the finale. More characteristically, women wait at home weaving and unweaving while the men have all the fun. They exist to be saved in the final scene.

Even the stories like Samuel Richardson's *Clarissa* (1748) or Hardy's *Tess of the d'Urbervilles* (1891) show the men as actors and deciders.[21] The women are the chosen and manipulated, requiring manly protection. Certainly such art has been a reflection of life. Few middle-class women before the twentieth century found socially acceptable means to support themselves outside of dependence on men. Two exceptions, however, appear in early fiction. They are Moll Flanders (from Daniel Defoe's novel by the same name) and Becky Sharp (from William Makepeace Thackeray's *Vanity Fair*).[22] Published in 1722 and 1847 respectively, these two novels feature the rare female rebel who refuses to bow to society or to settle for boring or repellent choices. Such independent women are perceived as tramps, unfit to mingle with decent folk, yet these judgments are partly the result of a strong double standard regarding male and female behavior. Whereas the sexual promiscuity presented in Henry Fielding's *Tom Jones* (1749) is perceived as a charming example of a young lad sowing his wild oats,[23] not so for Moll: she is a slut. Heroism or rebellion—or even unconventional behavior—except in rare cases, is not for women. Even in Christian novels, such as John Bunyan's *Pilgrim's Progress,* the good woman is not the risk taker. She stays behind, waiting to see if her man makes the journey that each Christian must make alone. Then, when he has reached The Celestial City, she reluctantly follows his lead.

Novels generally reflect the values of their audiences, telling us what those people in that time and place understood and accepted to be vices and virtues. The morality is not equally appropriate in such novels for men and for women. Yet surely the Christian must wonder whether modesty or chastity should not be as attractive in men as in women. Why are the moral young men in fiction perceived as funny and the chaste maidens viewed as charming? Surely moral values should be without gender. And in like manner, the ideals of heroism should not apply to men only—certain women are noted for types of heroism. As people have different obligations and roles in life, their virtue and villainy tend to grow from these life situations. But lying, cheating, sexual indulgence, abuse of others—these can apply to men and women alike. The Christian tradition in this is clearly one that demands high standards of both men *and* women.

Breaking Away

A few writers chose not to write traditional novels about traditional heroines. An early example is *Jane Eyre,* Charlotte Brontë's famous novel published in 1847.[24] Jane Eyre is a woman who makes her decisions with remarkable independence of spirit. She determines for herself, within those limitations that the world has forced upon her, the kind of life she will live. At the end, she chooses her vanquished lover Rochester as he had earlier chosen her. Her struggles with certain religious concerns are intrinsic to her actions, but she is no traditional Victorian moralist. Love matters more than social standing, courage more than conformity.

This is the Amazon figure emerging in women's literature, a figure that appears in several of the novels by Ellen Glasgow. In *Barren Ground,* a novel about a "fallen" woman, we see an untraditional heroine who picks herself up and works to make her life a success after this early failure in love. Although the mood of the story is vengeful, the triumph comes when she is released from her need for vengeance. At the end of the novel, when she again meets the lover, she discovers that she is much stronger and more successful than he. Her hatred melts into pity. But this is no Christian charity we see; rather it is the triumphant delight in having won a long fight, knowing that it is now possible to help the opponent off the ground. In this woman we observe a heroine who is not afraid to farm the ground, keep the account books, ride horses in all kinds of weather, and work from dawn till dusk.

No fragile flower of the Confederacy, this heroine is more like Scarlett O'Hara of Margaret Mitchell's later southern novel, *Gone with the Wind.* She is tough and victorious. Again, while not admirable within a Christian moral framework, she certainly is in the world created by the novelist. And she is presented to us for our grudging admiration.

A Voice of Her Own

A more dramatic and comic effort by Erica Jong recently won considerable critical acclaim. *Fanny* is the bawdy account of a woman who becomes a highway robber and a pirate in the tradition of the eighteenth-century picaresque hero.[25] She is a spoof on Moll Flanders, Defoe's somewhat more feminine heroine, who uses her beauty to manipulate men into doing her will. Jong's character does not need to manipulate others because she does so many things herself. She is quite capable of handling a gun or a horse.

However interesting and entertaining Fanny might be, she is neither a convincing portrayal of a real person nor a satisfying model of human conduct. Men who brandish swords and shout obscenities and play fast and loose with the ladies are not especially attractive to the morally alert reader. Women are no more attractive when they go into the same line of work. In most cases the woman-as-hero is a moral clod. The author, in an effort to convince, is too often inclined to delight in assertiveness and economic success. The bright young woman who proves herself tough as nails and climbs over all of her competitors to reach the top of the heap is no better or more ethically admirable than her male colleague in the gray flannel suit. Babbitt can be either male or female. Novels need not be preachy, and they need not conform to the reader's moral code. But the reader has the right and the responsibility to recognize and to judge both explicit and implicit values of the tale.

An Authentic Voice

The last of Spiller's categories is the discovery of the authentic voice. For Americans in general this occurred when our writers broke free from European forms and subjects and wrote of that which is uniquely American. Walt Whitman sang of the land and of the people in his own brazen voice; Nathaniel Hawthorne delved into the heart of American religion; and Herman Melville explored the deep mystery of whaling and the sea. Each of these authors found something in his own rich American experience that proved worth saying to a waiting world.

A parallel experience exists for modern women. When we are free of judgments and forms and subjects that men have built for us over the years, we can stitch a new art to fit our own experiences. But first we must go through the painful process of studying and understanding that experience. It will take many efforts to discover new ways of expressing the new insights. For now, we should expect to see much clumsy and obvious writing. Most great art grows out of many blots and erasures. It takes a combination of great talent with rich insights, the craft of expression and the power of imagination, a sympathetic and responsive audience—all at the right moment. We seem to be poised now for just such an experience.

Emily Dickinson spoke in an authentic voice. She wrote of gardens and snakes and carriages, of sewing and flowers and families—those things that she knew. Her voice was simple and clear and fresh. She made no effort to describe experiences that she had neither had nor could easily imagine. Limited—as was Jane Austen—to two square inches of ivory, she traced her lines on it with precision. Her rhythms are those she enjoyed in church songs, her images are those of her cloistered life. But she found the abridged life can be replete with imagination and can even contain moments of ecstasy.

For women today surely the artist herself remains the key to authenticity: her ability, her sensitivity to that gift, her steward-ship of her art. Twisting it to fit the morality of the masses, cutting her pattern to match the newest fad—such service of the marketplace sells books but erodes and prostitutes talent. The authentic voice is dictated by no human power outside of the artist: she knows what she has experienced, what has touched her deeply, what feels right. Like the potter centering her clay on the wheel, she knows intuitively when she is working well. The product that we enjoy reflects this centering in experience, in knowledge, in appropriate form. Even when the product is modest, the well-crafted work reaches out to us as an aesthetic experience.

How shall we know such a voice when we hear it? Much of this book deals with sensing the kind of person speaking, the language itself, the form, and the message that she is trying to share through her literature. Now we may look more closely at the author, then at the art itself, and finally at the message aimed through the art at the audience.

chapter three

Portrait of the Artist as Woman

The author discusses the scarcity of women artists throughout history and its roots in religious tradition, concluding that the limits placed on women's creativity are of human, not divine, origin.

Why didn't a woman write the plays of Shakespeare or the epics of Homer or the sonnets of Milton? Why are there so few women writers? Why are there so few masterpieces by women? Why are the major women writers clustered in such a short period of literary history, in such a few countries? Do women simply lack the talent and imagination that male artists have displayed over the generations?

Actually these provocative questions are secondary to our purposes in this study. The primary questions we should be asking are: What is creation? Is it different from making? What is inspiration? Is the artist in any way different from the craftsperson? Can a woman be an artist? Why do any of us write? Does the woman artist have different reasons from the man?

When we have defined such elusive terms as *art* and *artist* to our satisfaction and when we have determined whether these terms have any relationship to woman, then we can turn to the

39

cultural forces that affect creativity. This in turn can lead us to some idea of the appropriate conditions for nurturing that "authentic voice" we discussed earlier.

Creativity

Theories and practices of artistic creativity grow out of one's larger world view. For example, artists in the Judeo-Christian tradition tend to see themselves in the image of God. He proved the power of the Word. He said, "Let there be light," and there was light. He can bring something out of nothing. He can take primal chaos and give it order. And He knows us and can communicate with us because we are like Him. He created us in His image—male and female.

This dual image of the Creator as Artist and the artist as creator is particularly powerful, implying order and light and goodness. The new creatures—the works of this Creator—have integrity and liveliness and freedom.[26]

By contrast, we see much of the ancient world—especially Greece and Rome—more convinced of the truth of the pagan creation myths, often centering on the activities of that creatrix, the Mother Goddess. She was known by different names in different cultures—Cybele or Ashtoreth or Diana—and even the Jews knew the myths of this well-known symbol of physical fertility.

Hebrew literature is full of tales of prophets chopping away at the groves of Ashtoreth, the Canaanite goddess of fertility and war. And at Ephesus Paul, too, had his confrontations with disciples of Diana—the Roman version of the Great Mother.[27] Diana has always had her worshipers. No one would need to say, "Thou shalt have no other gods before me," if no other gods even offered threats to Jehovah's proper worship. The commandment makes no sense unless the people had some temptation to turn to other gods. Jesus reiterated this commandment, again demanding total allegiance to the one true God.

In the springtime, when the earth comes back to life, many are tempted to a heathenish celebration of the renewal of Mother Earth. In pagan myth this is Proserpine coming back from Hades to spend the next six months above ground with her mother, the goddess of the harvest.[28] Most of us are inclined to bend slightly in some fashion to the siren voice of this ancient goddess. The Greek folk celebrated the birth of spring with wine festivals—bacchanals. American youth too often echo the Hellenic culture, taking a spring vacation filled with alcohol and sex. This is the meaning of the tempting song of the Mother Goddess, the indulgence of our baser nature.

But for the artist, this creatrix is the force of irrational abandon, neither moral nor rational. From the outset, her advocates have tied her rites to nature worship, encouraging the sisterhood of worshipers who cherish darkness and fecundity. The modern daughters of Lilith recommend witchcraft, seeking recognition of the primacy of the female principle. And for the modern artist who races after this principle of chaos, this goddess of abundance and exaggeration, the path of art is violently romantic. Some modern poets echo the Dionysian revels of the Greeks, seeking through the stimulation of the body to transcend rational control.[29] Others believe in a kind of natural pattern—meandering without selectivity or judgment. Both are children of Ishtar/Diana.

Different cultures have cherished quite different notions of the artist and of art. While the Hebrews were given prohibitions against making graven images and bearing false witness that seemed to rule out sculpture or painting or the writing of fiction, they had a veneration for poetic and prophetic utterance. But songs and proverbs were perceived as God-created. The speaker or singer—and later the writer—was simply a conduit through whom God spoke to His people. The artist was not as important, the message was all-important.

Greek ideas of inspiration tended to be somewhat similar. Homer called for the help of the muses as he told his stories, which he claimed to be historical records. Later, Plato argued that the poet was not a rational "maker" of literature but an inspired madman who was in the thrall of the gods. The great plays of the Greek theater were a part of their worship service, in which the playwrights, the actors, and the audience all saw themselves as a part of the service.

Little purely secular literature has survived from these ancient cultures, perhaps because it lacked the mystical significance that would encourage scribes or believers to preserve it. The sacred texts of a people deserve commitment to memory and the risk of

41

life. And perhaps the very sacredness of such literature explains why women were not involved in its creation. In those cultures which exclude women from an active role in the worship service, we often find them also excluded from the arts.

Craft and Art

The explanation of female exclusion is by no means simple and uniform across cultures. Greeks did have goddesses and priestesses, but rarely female artists. It may be that Greek education, like the Hebrew, excluded women (at least decent women), so that the creations of women were more likely to have been in the more useful arts. In the golden age of Greece the sculptors and painters were seen as artisans, not artists. Although we might judge much of their pottery as art, the Greeks tended to value it as craft. Art was identified as a work of inspiration (the head), craft as a work of skill (the hands).

Assuming the Hebrew concept of inspiration, the artist as God's vessel, we can see the problem facing the creative woman. The religious community would consider woman too lowly a handmaiden to serve the sovereign God.

Mainstream religious groups have traditionally quoted from the account of Adam and Eve in the Garden of Eden (Gen. 2), not from the first creation narrative (Gen. 1). Relying on the standard interpretation of the event, they have pronounced through the ages that woman is a secondary, derivative creation, properly subject to man. Even so late an author as Milton, echoing the words of Paul as they appear in his letters to Timothy, to the Corinthians and elsewhere, saw woman as a secondary figure in God's creation. "He for God, and she for God in him," was his unforgettable phrasing of this received idea of hierarchy.

According to such tradition, woman was not allowed to lead in religious ceremonies. Nor should woman even speak in public worship; instead, she should wait patiently and then quietly ask questions of her husband, who supposedly would be able to interpret for her. Notice this may cause one to presuppose (as has commonly been the case) that the man has the theological training and that the woman is ignorant. The man was to be the thinker, the spokesman, the writer. The learned professions and the creative ones were the proper spheres of man. Woman's role was to support him in his endeavors by providing for his physical and emotional needs. She was to be the faithful helpmeet who traditionally stands behind every important man. And she was to be the hovering homemaker who keeps the children out of the way so that the great man can be the artist.

Part of this limitation set on woman has been a result of the doctrine of the Fall and of the notion that man sinned *because of* woman. In addition, the female creation has been subtly diminished by the preponderantly masculine imagery that surrounds God. Paraphrases, such as *Good News for Modern Man,* are particularly likely to be more gender specific than the original Scripture—as the very title would suggest.

Scripture is the bedrock of Christian faith. It is the conduit God frequently uses to speak to us. We cannot afford to have its language less than accurate. For one dedicated to the Christian faith, no study should matter more than a thorough grounding in Scripture.

Unfortunately, it is often claimed that the translators' slanted gender identification of neutral words has driven some of the radical feminists to abandon scriptural text entirely. In 1895 Elizabeth Cady Stanton started *The Woman's Bible,* a free-wheeling revision that simply altered those portions of Scripture identified by her as an affront to women.[30] The following year, the National American Woman Suffrage Association repudiated the effort. (Considering that Stanton was cofounder of the group, this was a painful rejection.) More current history has seen a new attempt at the free revision: the recently published "nonsexist" lectionary released by the National Council of Churches.

The Christian answer—at least for those who hold with biblical inerrancy—is that no one has a right to tamper with the text of Scripture. We can try explanations and paraphrases, but the original text is our best reference. This is God's Word, not a diving board from which one jumps to his or her own prejudices. What we need is to study Scripture in its entirety, not as a series of proof-texts to shore up our prejudices. We need solid scholarship. If God is as all-knowing and His Word as rich as we profess to believe, He will provide the ability to find the answers for those willing to study and think.

In the meantime, as arguments go on, the faith and language

both suffer change. As we learn more about gender identification of words, our terms sound awkward, our phrases clumsy. But we cannot ignore the importance of social assumptions behind word choices. Just now, graceful phrasing is not nearly so important as sensitivity to the human issues behind our word choices in translations *and* interpretations. As we shall see later in the discussion, this new sensitivity to sexist bias in language has enormous implications for literary creations.

The deeper issue of God's gender also has extensive implications for the artist. Some assume that Christ's manhood and His choice of men for disciples testify to man's *superiority* over woman. This in turn reinforces the old idea that only men should be ministers and priests and creative artists.[31] Women, from Miriam's day forward, have been allowed to bake the shewbread and weave the tapestries for the tabernacle. But they have had little or no right to participate actively in the more public life of the synagogue or church.

The inferior role of women reinforces the inferior status of women's work. Weaving of tapestries and embroidering and sewing and pottery making and basket weaving are perceived as useful and life enhancing, but of limited intellectual or spiritual concern. They are not valued as art, regardless of the artisan's degree of expertness. In the past the creative work that women did was likely to be classed with the "craft" performed by common laboring people, as noted in the discussion of Greece. (Actually, most artists recognize that craft is the competence that precedes most art and is essential to it.) Art moves to a higher level, requiring intellect and inspiration and demanding an aesthetic response. These were assumed to be more appropriate to men.

The Incarnation—The Word Made Flesh

The earthshaking change in the idea of art came with the Incarnation. The Word was made flesh, giving value to words and to begetting and to the flesh. Early Christians moved quickly into those areas prohibited to the Jews—visual arts and fiction. Their parables and statues and paintings blended culturally accepted form with Christian subject matter.

Jesus taught us that there is no primary or secondary in the kingdom of God. The first here shall be the last in God's kingdom. The emphasis on hierarchy and proper roles is a particular interpretation of God's purposes that is unnecessary for the body of Christ to function as He intends. Jesus never had to worry about His image, and He therefore never had to fret about women being kept in their place. He told Martha that her place was with Him. When God chose a lowly handmaiden as a suitable vessel for Himself, He thereby elevated womankind. The curse was shattered. So was the ancient prohibition on the arts.

Christ's life and character, the event of the Incarnation, and a full reading of the Gospels support the idea of the woman's full humanity and worthiness. It was to woman that God spoke in the Annunciation. He did indeed inspire her with His voice and entrust her with the seed of life that was to be His only Son. This new creation, echoing some aspects of the original creation and of the creative experience known by artists, lays to rest the arguments about the woman's potential for artistic inspiration. As God tells Peter later in the dream on the rooftop, man should not call unclean that which God has called holy. Whether dealing with food or Gentiles or women, the Christian era was to alter radically the pattern of Hebrew thought.

The Incarnation, then, made the role of women different from that time forth. Mary bowed to God's will and became the mother of the Messiah, a partner with God in a way that man has never known. Through her partnership with God, the Word was made flesh. Certainly this is the central mystical creative moment, overshadowing all other human experiences. The New Testament is specific on this act as a "begetting" rather than a "creation." The God-Man did not come *ex nihilo*. Thus the Incarnation becomes central to a new definition of the creative act. And by His partnership with woman in this act, God forever erased the old image of the unworthy vessel. *Of course* the woman in Christ can be a creative artist—she can be anything *God* wants her to be!

The Invisible Artist

Having discussed the Christian view of the arts and the role of the woman as artist, we are still left with the issue of why women have written so little so late.

Scholars have found that in some cultures and in some periods women have been encouraged to indulge in the production of certain art forms and have been dissuaded from others. For example, we find comparatively few women writers in the Greek world. In most anthologies the works of the great lyrical poetess Sappho (born ca. 610 B.C.) appear, but no others.[32] No women appear to have written the great tragedies or comedies. In fact, the actors themselves all appear to have been males—even when playing women's parts. Our anthologies chronicle no women poets to compete with Virgil or Lucretius or Horace in Roman culture. And again, the list of Roman playwrights includes no women's names. The medieval world is also strangely silent on the creative activities of women—though we do know of a few talented nuns who wrote plays and poems in imitation of the Latin masters.[33] From the eloquent and interesting letters and other documents that have survived, we suspect that much of the writing of women found no contemporary sponsors or audience or attention that would have given it prestige. Some of the fault clearly lies in the derivative nature of anthologies, where gleaners replicate the prejudices of their predecessors, a problem now being addressed by feminist scholars. But we must also assume that the men of artistic distinction outstripped the women by impressive odds. We must also therefore assume that custom, education, opportunity, or native ability was lacking.

In *The Obstacle Course* Germaine Greer suggests a provocative parallel with women and the visual arts: she believes many paintings attributed to men were at least partially painted by women. For example, the daughter, wife, or mistress of the artist would help paint some detail or background, but she would never receive or expect to receive credit. Just as the students of a master are not named until they do their own separate work, these women were the silent partners in the works of the masters. We wonder whether women helped their male relatives write their epics or plays.

This appears to be true to some extent even today. When a major historian such as Will Durant acknowledges the substantial contribution of his wife, one can easily surmise the contributions of female friends and relatives to the works of other well-known figures. And we suspect that in many cases where credit is finally given, much of the work and research on prior projects may have been done by this previously anonymous contributor, but will remain unacknowledged. Germaine Greer gives numerous examples to substantiate this.[34]

Virginia Woolf also suggests that "Anonymous" was a woman.[35] The lullabies and ballads of the medieval world, full of pain and love and violence, strike her as the natural creations of nameless women. All of this speculation is tempting. If creative women finally did surface, we must assume that the potential always existed but was rarely tapped. This is true of many men as well. The enormous waste of human potential is an enduring source of distress to those who love art.

From the time that the daughters of Eve went nameless, while the sons of Adam were named, the woman has frequently remained an anonymous member of the community. Veils and covers, harems and towers, have kept the faces from view. A recent book on growing up in the Chinese culture, *The Woman Warrior,* is a vivid modern example of this "invisible woman" syndrome.[36]

Although different ages have had different attitudes toward the publicity afforded an artist, most cultures have been consistent on the view that a modest, decent woman should refrain from exhibitionism. The male artist in the medieval world was frequently nameless, supposedly out of his desire to write or paint, not for personal glory, but instead for the greater glory of God. The female artist, until quite recently, has been nameless because society has usually disapproved of the public woman. The actress of the eighteenth century or the novelist of the nineteenth often struck her contemporaries as being aggressive, assertive, and immodest. Such behavior presents a problem for any Christian. The egocentric role of the modern artist contradicts Christ's promise of blessedness to the meek. Milton noted that pride—the celebration of self—is the "last infirmity of the noble mind."

Those few ages that have cherished artistic talent in woman have usually preferred that it be conformist and useful. A piece of embroidery that embellishes the household, a quilt that warms the children, a piece of cloth that adorns the church—these have been viewed as the proper products of woman's hands. The family can attribute the work to this artist, but the outside world would have little or no occasion to see the work or know her identity. For the most part, woman herself has been seen *as* the work of art—not a worker *in* the arts. Activists and public figures like Mary Wollstonecraft (feminist and mother of Mary Shelley, the poet's second wife) or the Grimke sisters were seen as misfits.[37]

As Virginia Woolf suggested, Shakespeare's fictitious sister would have found herself thwarted in a variety of ways. She would have had little chance for the education that marked the Renaissance gentleman. She would have learned even less Latin and no Greek. She would have been encouraged, while still in her teens, to marry a propertied neighbor who could give her a comfortable life. If she had protested that she loved poetry, she would have been told to forget such foolishness. For Shakespeare marriage was a temporary distraction that delayed his trip to the big city. For his imagined sister it would have been the work of a lifetime. She could not have left home and children to go off to Londontown. And if she had, she could not have apprenticed herself to a theater company to learn stagecraft. She could not have mingled freely with the men of London so as to acquire the stuff of which literature is made—the great breadth of human experience. Talent without opportunity or encouragement or hope of fruition is talent thwarted.

For a man like Milton, whose blindness and physical limitations threatened to be a barrier to his active life,[38] such frustration appeared to be a living death. He had to break out of this prison and express the great poetry that lived in his mind. And he was able to do this.

For women through the centuries the cultural barriers that have blocked the full use of their minds and talents also have often seemed a living death. The refusal to acknowledge their craft or to celebrate their art led some to madness. The refusal of publishers to publish their works and to recognize their ideas has been an incalculable loss to humankind. It is one kind of a sin to deny a calling that one feels strongly. It must be a far darker one to keep another person from her (*or* his) own proper work. Part of the woman's anguish lay, in part, in the fact that so often the thwarting was done by those who loved her and did it "for her own good."

Speaking Out

The path to publication—to making public our ideas—has been a rocky one for women. In the Renaissance world, when artists were increasingly celebrating their individuality and enjoying public recognition, most women continued to remain shadow figures. (Queen Elizabeth was an exception here—a woman of considerable learning and talent, who was quite open about her own abilities.) Women were rarely the authors of love lyrics. Courtly men wrote songs for them, asking that they "Come live with me and be my love." Their role was to sit demurely, looking like rosebuds that the men were to enjoy before their beauty was overblown. Or they were fruit, ripe for the picking—and no sooner ripe than rotten, according to some seventeenth-century writers. An object to be enjoyed, not a subject capable of joining in the enjoyment or inviting men to join her—this was the situation of the lovely lady of Renaissance literature.

Nor do women seem to have written many of the essays and plays of the eighteenth century. Yet in this era, some faint echoes of the female voice were heard in the literary world. Women were reading more and writing more. Gradually they achieved some modest recognition as the new form—the novel—grew in popularity. From the beginning, novels have been by, for, and about women to a startling degree. It is a private form, usually written not spoken, read not recited. It allows a degree of anonymity as well as privacy to the writer and to the reader. And it belongs to woman as does no other literary form (except perhaps the lullaby).

This literary genre does not demand the concentrated classical education of the older forms—the odes and epics and tragedies. The novel relies more on life experience and on passion and native talent. Middle-class men like Daniel Defoe and Samuel Richardson wrote of the middle-class experience. And they discovered that their great reading public were primarily women. By the eighteenth century, lending libraries had also made literature more widely available to women of all classes. These women quickly learned to copy the forms that they read.

In its style the novel is close to conversation and to letter writing. It is not surprising that one of the first novelists of the

49

seventeenth century was a woman. By the nineteenth century, France had George Sand and England had George Eliot, both prolific *female* novelists, passing as men for the benefit of the reading public. But others were clearly not just women, but ladies of the middle class who acknowledged their femaleness and their authorship. Jane Austen (1775–1817), author of *Emma, Pride and Prejudice, Sense and Sensibility,* and other great works, comes readily to mind as an example of the artist who is supremely accomplished in her art and feminine in her person. There were numerous other female writers of the same caliber in the nineteenth century.[39]

Virginia Woolf claimed that most women writers have been single and childless. Others have argued that she exaggerated this. Certainly, many modern writers are mothers. Woman's role as mother has tended to substitute for and to interfere with the creative role as author. Whether in the physical process of reproduction or the far more extended and more emotionally draining process of nurturing, women have spent themselves for their children. The demands of repeated childbearing once resulted in early death. The weariness and busyness of caring for children allowed little space for mothering-forth literature. As Woolf noted, the absence of a room of one's own and of time for writing is clearly a powerful enemy to the creative urge.

In a more positive sense, dedicated mothering draws on the reservoir of creativity that also serves literature. After an imaginative afternoon with children, sharing stories and activities, following their ideas and leading out to fresh perspectives and values that the mother wishes to reinforce, a woman is not only spent, she is satisfied. She no longer has that hunger for creative expression that drives the lonely recluse to put her pen to paper. She may be content to rock before the fire, telling her husband about the day she has spent with the children. Literary creativity does grow, in part, from a discontent, a hunger. In some ways, good friends and good family relations are the enemies of any writer—they allow her to use up her powers in creative living.

History was to feed discontent for a number of years, to the detriment of marriage and the benefit of literature. In the nineteenth and twentieth centuries, when time and space became more plentiful, social pressures interfered. The average middle-class woman has been encouraged over the years to use her time in serving God and man, not the muses. She was to do good works, to ply her needle, to visit the poor, to tend to household management. Some light reading was encouraged for her pleasure and to provide topics for social intercourse. She was also encouraged to occasional writing as well, as long as it did not tire her or make her nervous. The social arts of the Victorian age were for private entertainment or for family and friends. The man, not the woman, was to be the public person. The woman belonged to the household. Yet Jane Austen and other nineteenth-century women found their voices and spoke out clearly and seriously and professionally. They also found a public.

All of this sounds very hopeful. But it is well to recall that Sylvia Plath, a modern poet and novelist, writes in *The Bell Jar*[40] of subtle stresses that continue to make even modern adolescent girls feel they must choose between marriage and careers. The boys, on the other hand, *assume* that they can do both. And when the children come, the talented woman may become schizophrenic in her love of them, her guilt at time spent apart from them, and her ache to write. Though she loves her children, they may not always be enough to satisfy her intellectual and creative urges.

Certainly the act of bearing children is the unique blessing and burden of woman. But for a woman, as for a man, creativity may take a form broader than the simple biological act of childbirth. The nurturing of the child, the cultivation of spiritual values, is a demanding experience and a thrilling one that is to be shared by both mothers and fathers. Like men, women may sometimes want to leave something in addition to children to mark their passage through this world. When children fill the home, they fill the heart and mind as well, leaving little space for other interests. But modern Western life with more limited families can allow for artistic life as well.

Ellen Glasgow preaches fervently for life beyond the home. In *Virginia* she tells a bitter story of a woman who uses all of her creativity and attention on her home. The heroine, Virginia, has been carefully prepared for the strictly limited role of providing for man's needs and for his children's. After a lifetime of unthinking adherence to the creed that claims clothes and food and bodily health are the only proper concerns of woman, she wakes one day to find her house empty. The children have flown the tidy nest, and her husband wants more than an evening meal. Bored with her mindless domesticity, he turns to a more vivacious woman, an actress who has spent her life creating roles and finding a voice for her talents. Such a rude recognition scene has greeted many middle-aged housewives in recent years— especially since divorce has become increasingly socially acceptable. Dreams must be large enough to encompass an entire life. Women must grow and mature just as men do, or they are doomed to an old age of being tolerated rather than enjoyed, of waiting for visitors rather than planning adventures.

Like men, women find that writing books can provide one kind of physical immortality. Books are satisfying in the sense that, through them, we can communicate with future generations. Too often women's work seems hopeless and repetitive: the dust on the piano will outlive us and all our petty efforts; the clothes will be dirty and rumpled almost as soon as we put them back in the closet; and the dinner that takes five hours to cook is eaten in five minutes. Just as we glow at the idea that our children will carry our values beyond our limited lives, that in them we have accomplished something fine and enduring, so we can delight in imagining our words reaching out in time and space, touching people we shall never meet.

Books are also satisfying to women for their ability to communicate. Frequently women feel isolated in their work. The older communities allowed families to share their homes and their working places with other generations and with neighbors. The consequence, then, of having a house in the suburbs and a room of one's own may be isolation. Through the written word, we can enjoy listening to voices other than those of the coffee klatsch and the PTA, we can speak to people who are not members of the local church, and we can discuss ideas that no one in the family finds worth bothering about. Books are a rich form of liberation of the mind and spirit.

Actually, the modern world is full of examples of women with husbands *and* families *and* writing careers. The burdens of motherhood were exaggerated by the childless Woolf. A supportive husband (as Woolf herself discovered in her husband, Leonard) can make life quite comfortable for a creative woman. She needs to set aside time for her own work from the moment she marries. Under the right circumstances, the experiences of being a wife and mother provide exciting subjects for discussion (witness the works of modern family-oriented writers Jean Kerr and Erma Bombeck). In such cases a writer's life can inform her work rather than subvert it. No longer need we make an absolute choice between motherhood and artistic endeavor. The late emergence of the mother-writer may account for the paucity of mature heroines and the consequent rich stories of family life. Even women writers have commonly written of young heroines and their love affairs; now they are beginning to write more about childbearing and the ecstasy and agony of family life.

Finding a Woman's Proper Work

Even beyond the concerns for filling our time, making our husbands and our children happy with our versatility, and seeking to leave footprints on the sands of time, creative women are responding to a basic human need—to find their own proper work. Dorothy L. Sayers notes that the sanctity of work encompasses a significant portion of the creation narrative. It is unfortunate that the Fall gave such a bad name to work. Even before the Fall, Adam and Eve had work assigned by God. They were to tend the garden. Built into every human being is the fundamental appetite for meaningful work. Without a satisfying means of using our talents, we feel enormously frustrated. Enforced leisure is no pleasure. Obviously not all of us are driven to the same level of activity. Some can indeed make their work expand to fill the time available. All of us have seen people work at such a pace—whether the homemaker pinning up clothes on the line with absolute precision, ironing wash-and-wear fabrics, shelling peas laboriously; or the business clerk shuffling papers and sharpening pencils until the clock strikes 5:00 P.M. But others see time as precious and work as important. Such women may grow so angry and frustrated that they appear grotesque to the plodding world around them.

A number of biographies of creative women in the nineteenth century—the Brontës, Emily Dickinson, Christina Rossetti, and others—point to the alienation such women may feel. *The Madwoman in the Attic* (a recent literary history) is the study of women artists who were perceived as eccentric by the Victorian culture.[41] Even as the society, grudgingly and gradually, acknowledged the abilities of women, it stereotyped its creative women as mental and social misfits.

The era had little tolerance for the so-called New Woman who was emerging. Political, educational, and economic forces in the nineteenth century allowed women—especially single women—to become nurses or missionaries or teachers or political activists or writers. Their escape from the traditional parlor or nursery or kitchen puzzled many English citizens. The concept of a woman's place and the need to keep all women in their proper place made women like George Eliot or Charlotte Brontë seem rebellious. Their deviation from mainstream thought brought on a sense of alienation that undoubtedly contributed to their warping—a kind of self-fulfilling prophecy.

In America a good example of this pressure to conform is evident in the life of Alice James. A recent prize-winning biography by author Jean Strouse shows how this bright woman grew up in a home full of independent and talented people. One brother was Henry James, the novelist. Another was William James, the philosopher and psychologist. Neither they nor their father ever expected Alice to amount to anything. She was a woman and consequently doomed to being adored or ignored. Denied useful labor, she turned her energy and talent into self-destruction. Nervous ailments and constant pleas for attention made her a family burden. Though she never married, she also never wrote for publication. No one stopped her, but no one encouraged her either. Toward the end of her life, when she knew that she had cancer and that her complaints were at last justified in the eyes of a weary world, she kept a diary. This poignant document discloses her sense of uselessness and pain. These few pages suggest that she too had talent and brains. But the chance to use them died with her. What remains is the chronicle of a wasted life.

A totally different nineteenth-century American story, that of a woman who refused to confine herself to Victorian expectations, is the life of Charlotte Perkins Gilman. She rejected what *she* considered the mindless wifely role to become a writer, economist, and political activist. Her contemporaries condemned her nonconformist life, including her abandonment of her husband and child, as a scandal. She could not live in the doll's house that the decent folk of the nineteenth century had built for the "good" woman. She felt society was insisting that she must choose between freedom and mental death.

In Gilman's nineteenth century the talented woman found herself completely at odds with her world. If she married, she was expected to do nothing other than raise her children and help her husband. In society she was to be seen and not heard, like an obedient child. In her novels *The Age of Innocence* and *The House of Mirth*,[42] American novelist Edith Wharton (1862–1937) portrays the stunted lives of such women and the high price they paid for nonconformity—a price Wharton herself was also obliged to pay. It took a strong woman to assert herself against the prevailing wisdom. And the subsequent individualism frequently seems more perverse than satisfying. Constant warfare is not conducive to graceful living or generous dispositions.

If a woman did not marry, she was usually considered a freak. She could become a "schoolmarm" or a nurse, jobs not held in high esteem by the society. Middle-class families expected their single daughters to stay at home, taking care of the house for an aging father, drinking tea with a few neighbors, and growing a few flowers.

Thus the woman who indulged her creative drives and made her productions public must have felt herself illicit and shameful. Writing was considered a subversive act. And any effort to publish was seen as both unfeminine and rebellious. It is only fair to note that upper-middle-class male authors were also discouraged from writing, and their work was seen also as subversive or peculiar. Writing—other than political manifestoes—seemed an inappropriate and frivolous activity for either the gentleman or the gentlewoman. Wharton, in fact, shows that her New York distrusted all artists. Few cultures through history have accepted the arts as suitable pursuits for respectable adults. The artist presumably runs up the rebel flag of Bohemia as soon as she puts pen to paper. Certainly the faddish turn-of-the-century model of the artist-as-rebel was to reinforce this suspicion among decent folks.

The twentieth century has grown more accustomed to the woman as artist and has been somewhat kinder to her. The twentieth century has finally broken free. The modern woman has opportunities available to her never before open in recorded history. Modern women, unlike Shakespeare's sister, may marry or not, select a college or an apprenticeship, see the world, combine workplace and marriage, have children or not. She can write whatever she likes, and with "luck" and a flair for ascertaining the public taste, she may even find a publisher and an eager audience. She is free at last to discover her truth and to speak out in her own voice—not a pale imitation or a shrill response, but an authentic and fully modulated voice.

God, the Archetypal Artist

The image of God is in every human being. If we recall the creation accounts in Genesis, we note that man (male and female) was created in the image of a creative God. The human came at the climax of a series of acts, after God had taken chaos and made it into order. The image of God is therefore a creative image, and the nature of the human is to be creative in a parallel manner. All of God's creatures were told to be fruitful; only humans were separated out to be fruitful in a spiritual way, not only through physical procreation. A significant part of the life of Christians is their rediscovery of God's original creativity in them and the nurturing of that spark.

God took clay and breathed life into it. Many artists feel that that is the act of artistic creation. In the beautiful fresco on the ceiling of the Sistine Chapel, Michelangelo pictures God reaching out to touch the finger of the inert Adam. The viewer can almost see the electricity between the two hands. Taking words or clay or paint and breathing life into them—this is the role of the artist. And it is a role that mirrors the life-giving touch of God Himself.

This is clearly a time for lively and legitimate arguments about the nature of man and woman, of the artist-writer, and of God. God, after all, is the archetypal Artist. The human is only a limited copy. Modern scholars have recently opened up a vast body of new linguistic and historical materials that deserve our consideration. The true believer should not fear honest study. If God is truth, surely His Word is true. An honest search can only reveal more and more of the invaluable insights that we all desire.

We need not join those who would confine woman in tightly

laced corsets of outdated prohibitions. Nor need we rip off all our clothes to join the new coven of witches hymning the beauties of Mother Earth. We need to forge a theology of women and creativity that liberates while holding firmly to the faith.[43] Our image of the new wine in old skins reminds us of the balanced requirements—tradition and flexibility. Most important, we need the spirit of the living God breathing through our forms—making all things new.

Without forms and rules, in life or in art, we have no basis for either craft or communication. An architect is bound by natural laws (such as stress) and by taste (the preference for arches or stone façades). A writer is also working within boundaries. She must use her words in a certain way if she expects to have readers. Yet if she slavishly cuts her garments to the pattern of those who preceded her, she is neglecting her own individual needs, and the dress will not fit. The real artist will take the form and bring new color and shape and life to it.

If indeed the Christian artist sees herself in the image of the creative God, she must be curious about the nature of that God she reflects. Genesis notes that God's image is male and female. Later Paul uses phrasing that echoes this, in saying that in Christ we are neither male nor female. Such disturbing and provocative phrases suggest something of the inclusive nature of God and His creatures. Samuel Taylor Coleridge, poet and critic during England's Romantic era, refers to the mind as the great androgyny. While for most of us our bodies are easily defined as having gender, he suggests that our imaginations do not. Many moderns have discussed this issue, whether there is an innate psychological difference between men and women, whether we are born with different kinds of brains and abilities. In her study *Toward a Recognition of Androgyny*, Carolyn Heilbroun insists that the creative mind is not limited by sexual identity, but transcends it.[44] Although the person may be constricted to the experience of one sex throughout life, claims Heilbroun, the mind is capable of extending beyond the individual experience and the individual sex.

We know that throughout history the creative intellect has repeatedly contained both feminine and masculine experience. The sensitive person can look at the pain on another's face and intuit the experience behind that expression. He or she can project into the other person's life and mind to live vicariously the life of another. This is, in fact, one of the great thrills of reading and writing, the chance to break out of our physical confinements.

It is therefore not surprising that some of the most eloquent early studies of women's concerns appeared in plays, poems, stories, and epics written by men. The writer by his very nature is inclined to be more sensitive than most, to look more closely at the people whom he describes. Among the Greeks, Euripides (fifth century B.C.) in particular was enormously sensitive to the woman's point of view. The tragedy of *Medea,* for example, displays a woman who by knowledge and will could act the role of the hero. But largely because of her sex, she was trapped into being the instrument of Jason's sport. She had been the cause of his salvation from her family at an earlier time; when she realized that he had cast her into a slave role, she became the instrument of his doom.

Geoffrey Chaucer, fourteenth-century English poet and author of *The Canterbury Tales,* presented the Wife of Bath as the most boisterous storyteller of all the Canterbury pilgrims. She is a woman full of the joy of living, who is thoroughly assertive in affairs of the heart. In the eighteenth century Defoe wrote at length in *Projects* about the need to educate women.[45] His novels are full of lively and exciting female characters. Then, in the nineteenth century, John Stuart Mill, English philosopher and political economist, revealed in *The Subjection of Women* close reasoning and sensitive understanding of the problems of the bright and talented woman.[46] It was, after all, another nineteenth-century man—Henrik Ibsen, a Norwegian play-wright—who provided the modern feminists with one of their favorite images, the doll's house.[47]

Over and over, men have spoken for women, defending their rights, arguing for their liberation, their right to a fulfilling and creative existence. The human imagination allows us to step out of our skins and to understand our neighbors.

Nor need the writing necessarily bear any marks of sexual identity. Readers who first studied Willa Cather's novels of the pioneers and the frontier found little to signify that this writer was a woman. The mind may indeed be androgynous for many artists.

Even so, most writers find their writing grows out of their own experience and consequently their own sexual identity. For those who do root their work in life, being male or female is enormously important. Many women would find it almost impossible to imagine what it is to fight a war or play football. Good writers acknowledge their limitations and use their special insights to communicate fresh ideas to others.

Our God transcends the physical, but alas—for the time being—we do not. His is the enduring truth that we seek to capture in our frail and transient words. He is indeed the archetypal Artist. When we seek to bring our chaotic thoughts into shape and express them creatively, we are acting out—in our small way—the original creation. When we take a form and try to breathe life into it, we are copying God. And when we give birth to either child or idea and nurture it, we recall the Incarnation.

As beings who bear the image of this creative God, we find satisfaction in acts of creativity that imitate His. Men and women both delight in making things new. We look at these creations and, like God, feel pleasure in seeing that they are good.

It has not been Scripture that has kept women from writing the plays of Shakespeare. The God of Scripture, whose image is both male and female, is creative and encourages creativity in His children. Christ encourages women to be all that they can be. The obstacles are mainly human constructs and perceptions. In breaking down our clichés about "woman's role" or "woman's nature," we must tear away only the humanly made foolishness. The foundation stone of our lives is still Christ.

Our God is sufficient.

chapter four

The Search for Form

The author traces the relationship between women and various forms of literature, showing how women gradually have made inroads into the literary world during the past few centuries. Particular attention is paid to the novel and its attraction for women both as writers and readers.

The artist is only *potentially* an artist unless she finds a form in which to express the ideas that people her imagination. Most of us have experienced this search for form in a private way. We come within inches of being hit by a car, and we grope for the right way to express our anger or fear. We grow weary of a relationship, and we either find a way to revive it or look for words to soften the breakup. We hear of a child's death, and we try to think how we can express sympathy to the parents. Each of us has needed to express some idea or emotion and has thought about the form that expression should take. "Fiddlesticks!" is not strong enough for the near accident. "Buzz off!" is not a kind way to leave someone we have loved. "Better luck next time," will not serve to comfort the bereaved parents.

Literary Form and Culture

Form is a combination of word choice, level of diction, tone, and structure. Even the more elaborate forms grow from simple human needs to communicate. For instance, we want to explain a process or argue a case, so we choose prose. We want to win someone's heart, so we choose poetry. Each culture develops its rituals and its attendant literary forms—the lament or the work song or the wedding march or the lullaby. Because we grow up with these forms all about us, they become an unconscious part of our expectations. Somehow we sense the appropriate way to express emotions and to phrase ideas.

A primitive people seeking to survive in the face of formidable odds builds stories of brute strength and of shrewd strategems. A more mature culture can handle life in more subtle and elegant ways. The audience that hears or sees or reads the work determines much of its shape. The artist must use a form that communicates, that comforts by its familiarity and delights by its originality. The shape of the work, as the ideas that are encapsulated in it, derives from multiple sources. The individual experiences are a part of history and of place and culture and timing. All of these build aesthetic conventions considered appropriate for artistic expression. The modern, college-educated American female will choose a very different form of expression from the primitive, aristocratic Greek male.

In fact, the most celebrated of the older art forms were intended for an aristocratic male audience. The bard chanted his epics to men who lounged about while eating and drinking. The tragic dramatist staged his plays for the men of Athens who sat on stone benches in the amphitheater. The Hebrew psalmist sang to men, the warriors and worshipers of Israel. Over the years, because of the educational and social structure, men have been the ones who have had the skills and education required for written literature. Usually it has been the men first who have been taught to read and to write. So it is mainly men the stories and songs have addressed. And it is the lives and interests of men that these stories have reflected.

Some slight change appears in the medieval world. The convents gave some women opportunities for literacy along with the peace of mind to do creative work. Therefore, out of the convents came religious plays that were written in the classical tradition and apparently performed for and by the nuns.[48] The medieval courts also encouraged a more elevated status and taste for women. Medieval storytellers characterize both men and women as tellers of tales. Chaucer's women on his pilgrimage are eager and able to contribute both pious and bawdy stories.

Literacy increased among women in the Renaissance, in part because of the Protestant zeal to teach every individual the means to read the Scripture for herself. In Elizabethan England the women joined the men in the audience of the great theaters— even if they were not the authors of the plays or the actors in the plays. Later, in the seventeenth century, when the first of the novels were written, women were among the first readers and writers of the novel. Studies that discuss the rise of the novel in England suggest that women had voracious appetites for this new form of writing early on. Physical changes, such as the increased size of middle-class homes and the consequent opportunity for privacy, and the increased availability of artificial light to prolong reading time—these helped enlarge the reading public. The cheaper editions and the lending libraries gradually made books accessible to lower classes. Servant girls in the eighteenth century, in their own chambers in the big houses, could indulge their need for adventure by reading about Moll Flanders or Clarissa. Women over the years have found literature a socially acceptable form of escape.

The Rise of the Novel—An Opportunity for Women

The novel, the new form that followed the loose and informal design of life itself, was to prove an exciting alternative for those whose own lives were tragically limited. Physically one might be constrained and hampered by ballooning skirts. Socially one might be limited by rigid rules of conduct and by the subservient and dreary life of the domestic servant. But in imagination, one could be a picaresque hero romping along the highways of England and sailing off to the New World in search of fortune.

Recognizing the appetite of this new literary audience, writers like Samuel Richardson told stories of servant girls who found their path to happiness through a shrewd adherence to virtue. His Pamela is one such character and a classic figure. She is a young and pretty maiden of a poor but honest family who finds herself at the mercy of a wealthy (and handsome) young master. She fights off his lecherous attacks, eludes his clever seductions, and finally wins his respect and love. Her wedding is a clear triumph of virtue over vice. In fact, the full title of this work is: *Pamela; or, Virtue Rewarded.* The book sold because her circumstances were so common and her success so uncommon.

Earlier Defoe had told the darker side of the same tale. Moll Flanders fell enthusiastically into the snares set by her young master and then married another son of the same family. After his death, she moved to a life of whoring and thieving. The story is told from the point of view of an old, supposedly penitent woman, full of moralizing interludes and erotic details. Defoe's obvious pleasure in Moll's lusty career belies his pretense at moral uplift. (Both novels dwell on dubious moral views and lead to questionable conclusions. Even eighteenth-century contemporaries quarreled with their commercial values and simplistic morality.)

Not all of the figures in these eighteenth-century novels were serving girls. Some were middle-class ladies who found their lives equally full of pitfalls. Clarissa, another of Richardson's heroines, refused to marry the repulsive man her parents tried to force upon her. After leaping to the alternative path of elopement with her suitor Lovelace, she repented of her haste, her choice, and her love. Her heroic defiance of her cruel parents resulted in her tragic death.

Eighteenth-century novelists found that female readers wanted to hear of youth and beauty and wealth and adventure and lust and danger and love—the stuff of twentieth-century romances as well. From the beginning, the novel has been the form that has attracted women writers as well as readers, and for many of the same reasons. Although more women in the eighteenth century had more education than ever before in history, it was rarely the "proper" education. Until quite recently, the proper education for the man of learning and wealth has been the classical one. The ability to quote from the odes of the Roman poet Horace or to reproduce passages from Homer by memory marked the gentleman. A lady learned enough to read, to write, and to cipher, but her attention was not on the classics. Rather a lady was "finished" by learning dancing and singing and sewing. Her concern was with manners and pleasing appearance. Having no expertise in the classics, she was less likely than the man to enjoy the subtleties of neoclassical elegance. For the uneducated the Horatian ode or the epic hexameter had no particular charm. Unable to read the original works, the lady could have no desire to produce any kind of translation or adaptation. But the novel was a genre that was wide open. It grew out of the insatiable appetite for life among the emerging middle class. It is a virtual amoeba of a genre, taking on the shape of the life within.

Women Settling Down to Write

One of the most famous of the early novelists was a Frenchwoman named Mme. Magdeleine de Scudéry.[49] She had joined the men with her writing of lengthy "key" novels that disguised and discussed the scandals of her day. She was immediately perceived as a free spirit with minimal morality. This connection of immorality and ambition and talent was to become the unfortunate stereotype of the female novelist for centuries. A woman writer, a female novelist, was by definition *no lady*.

The nineteenth century, however, did see the rise of more "ladylike" novelists. No one would accuse Jane Austen of leading a scandalous life. And no one could deny the immensity of her talent. With a clear mind and a sharp tongue, she satirized the life around her, writing with polish and taste. She never sought to write an epic—because that was not the nature of her talent. She wrote about that which she knew. And she knew thoroughly only the circumscribed life of the genteel maiden lady.

Born into the eighteenth century, Jane Austen wrote her few novels early in the nineteenth century. She was a clergyman's daughter in a small town in southern England. Though she is said to have been attractive and graceful with a talent for social dancing, she never married. She apparently enjoyed the life of the family, knew virtually nothing of the larger world, and rarely ventured more than a few miles away from home. It is remarkable that such a life could furnish the material for literature.

Other women followed Austen in significant numbers. The

nineteenth-century British landscape is full of women writers who developed psychological, social, and moral themes in their novels, which number in the thousands. Among the better-known names are the Brontës, Elizabeth Gaskell, and George Eliot. But lesser names abound in literary history.

Each of these had her own individual experiences. The Brontës, three girls and one boy, were from Haworth on the brooding Yorkshire moors. They too were the children of a clergyman. But they were far more isolated from social life than Austen. For compensation and entertainment they created their own make-believe world and peopled it with their own creatures of myth. Later all three of the girls were to write novels. But it was Charlotte Brontë who proved the most daring and who traveled the farthest.

Another nineteenth-century English lady, Elizabeth Gaskell, was fascinated by Charlotte Brontë and wrote the first biography of her. Like Brontë, Gaskell was a daring young woman. This respectable young matron stepped beyond the polite social life around her to chronicle, in addition, the sweeping social changes of Victorian England. She dared to write about the great world.

In another way, the far more scandalous George Eliot also enlarged the materials of women's literature.[50] Her life was as nonconformist as her pen name. For years she lived openly with a married man and faced the umbrage of a polite society that ostracized them both. She studied the new religious ideas current in Germany and wrote about "secular Christianity"—portraying Jesus as an ideal man rather than as God. She described herself (in *Mill on the Floss*) and her father (in *Adam Bede*). She loved to tell about her farm home, her neighbors, and her perceptions of human problems. Her novels about the poor country folk of England are handled with the fidelity to homey detail that we find in Dutch painting—loving and precise. And she did not hesitate to develop moral concerns and philosophic issues as they arose within the narrative.

Such women as these suggest the range of Victorian novelists. They wrote powerfully about many people, places, and ideas, and they were widely read and enthusiastically received by both men and women. Writing had become a career open to all women, and one that could pay a living wage.

The circumstances of writing are various, but the history of women's literature is the history of a search for privacy and peace—for a room of one's own. Jane Austen did her writing in the sitting room that was used by the entire family. She needed to be alone to do her work, and she resisted the curiosity of those who would look over her shoulder. For her the creaking door became the signal that an intruder was on the way. She would then cover her work and turn her attention to the life of the family.

Other authors speak at length of this problem. Erica Jong, for instance, tells of the need to find writing time and space apart from her husband and child. Today, such a successful writer can rent a room or a studio. But for other women, less successful, less assertive, this is out of the question.

From the time of those anonymous medieval authors, women have found that their physical circumstances controlled their opportunities for composition. A tribute to the indomitable imagination of the human is the consequent accommodation of the form to the circumstances. Some women found that they could carry a short lyric in the mind, making this a handy form for a busy person. The artist does not need large blocks of time or privacy to create such poetry. One can think about rhymes and rhythms off and on while washing or cooking or while rocking the baby.

Later, in the nineteenth century, New England poetess Emily Dickinson was to find that the actual writing of the poetry took private time. She had to wait until her demanding father was asleep to transcribe the poems that haunted her all day. She got up in the middle of the night and wrote her poems by candlelight.[51] More recently, Tillie Olsen, speaking about a black woman writing and thinking, records the meditations that she has while she is ironing.

Virginia Woolf pointed out that most writers need, in addition to education and space, an independent and regular income. Few women of the laboring classes have had the creative zeal left for composing sonnets after doing the diapers, the dishes, the weaving, the sewing, the milking, and the harvesting. In all fairness, laboring men have had much the same problem. Aside from Piers Plowman, Robert Burns, and Robert Frost, few poets even pretended to be farmers.

The nineteenth century gradually saw the encouragement of

middle-class writers, including some women. But more public and ornamental activities were considered appropriate for fine ladies. The Victorian lady was often seen as a fine piece of decor. If she was busy with her needle, her image as the cultural, sensitive, delicate gentlewoman was significantly enhanced. If the work was beautiful but useless, then the husband was portrayed as a good provider who could afford beauty and waste—conspicuous consumption, one might say. Ordinarily, the work done was praised beyond its quality. The lovely ladies were not expected to do more than produce the modest craft of the dilettante. But an occasional woman turned this frivolity into art. The willingness to take one's craft seriously is one more mark separating the artist from the dabbler.

Thus, the kind of portraiture or writing that a lady like Austen's Emma (from the work by the same name) might do to wile away the time gracefully does not compare with the real work of Mary Cassatt or Jane Austen. Because of a genuine love of beauty and a professional dedication to it, Christina Rossetti sang out her glorious lyrics and Elizabeth Barrett Browning penned her moving and provocative poems.

The twentieth century has seen a number of women writing both poetry and prose with increasing success. The educational advantages of the new century have taught women that classical forms are indeed accessible to them and powerful to use. They have therefore expanded the range of their poetry from the lyrics and lullabies and love songs. And they have expanded the range of their novels. Willa Cather, for instance, saw no reason to limit her novels to ladylike miniatures. Some of her Midwestern tales have epic scope.

The professional opportunities of these last few years have even begun to open up commercial theater to a handful of women playwrights. Lillian Hellman, a real power in American theater, writes plays that are by no means feminine. In fact, her ideas and characters are as clear and tough as those of any male author of her era. Although she and Sheleigh Delaney[52] and others of the new feminist theater have had some success, this is not a form available to most women. Lorraine Hansberry is even more remarkable with her Broadway successes. It is amazing to have an example of an author who is young and female and black and talented—and successful. Plays usually need to be produced. They are not a private form that can fill the days of a lonely spinster scribbling on the back of an envelope or a busy housewife catching a moment between chores. The production arrangements, the vast cast of professional producers, directors, scenery designers, painters, builders, orchestra, actors, costume designers, lighting designers—these are likely to terrify the amateur. By comparison, the novel, the short story, or the poem is much more natural and comfortable for the novice writer, male or female.

Given the twentieth-century taste for prose, it is predictable that women have preferred to write novels. The novel, as we have seen, was shaped for women and by women. It allows easily for alteration to fit the individual talent and needs. The novel can reflect women's rapidly changing attitudes, their newly emerging imagery, their altered concept of character, and their radically new language. The novel can be reflective or polemic or lyrical or angry or meditative or funny. Modern poetry has much of the same flexibility for writers. But contemporary taste makes the flexibility and consequent popularity of the short story and novel the most likely forms of expression for women. Writers prefer to have readers.

Within these forms and occasionally in others as well, modern women writers are finding that they can succeed. Their escalation to the forefront of modern literature has raised sensitivity to their concerns. And this in turn has changed the face of the literature. The increased understanding of women is clearly a direct result of the increased ability of women to articulate their ideas and feelings—to speak out clearly. They have, after thousands of years, a voice of their own at last.

Finding the Right Words

The forms of the literature depend most basically on the choice of words—the level and flexibility of the language available. We have already discussed the clumsiness of masculine/feminine language patterns. We are now in the process of radically changing the interpretation of words. This leaves us with an awkwardness in composition. If we cannot say "mailman," and we do not have the stomach to say "mailperson," we are stuck with avoiding the reference to that creature who is delivering the mail. The he/she usage quickly grows tiresome. Yet for the time being, we need the convention of asking that each man or woman express his or her thoughts as he or she chooses.

Other changes are actually freeing the language. The new feminine readers are helping us to consider the appropriateness of our images. Machine images (like "blowing a gasket") are often meaningless to both men and women. The new household images (a "mind like an unmade bed") are colorful and fresh—but a bit jarring for the present. Allowing the images of the bedroom, the kitchen, the laundry to become a part of literary speech opens up to us a whole buffet of delicious choices. When Dorothy L. Sayers says that Lord Peter is as "subtle as a can opener," we all picture the punctured can, the raw edges, and we see what she means. The image is crisp and clear. It communicates.

By using these new frames of reference, women can expand the speech, the pool of available imagery, and the sensitivity to women's daily lives. They then change the forms and the conventions.

Emily Dickinson showed us how a household could be the world for a woman. Jane Austen could make each word or gesture carry importance. Eudora Welty can draw history from the objects on a dresser. These women use the found objects of their world to symbolize whole clusters of history and ideas. Baking a coconut cake can be a gesture of love. Listening with attention to the details of an old lady's illness can show enormous patience and sensitivity and humanity. Women know the language of gesture, the symbolism of clothes, the significance of foods, the vocabulary of domesticity.

Great riches lie in store for us as we reveal the untapped folk wisdom and incredible sensitivity that often lie beneath a woman's apparently placid life. Traditional speech patterns will not serve to uncover these treasures. We need to take them ever so gently from their wrappings of silence and allow them a place of honor.

We live at a time when a folk language is finding literary form. Robert Burns sought a voice for his Scots dialect and his neighbors' eccentricities. His poetry broke radically from traditional British literary language and rhythms and images. Later black artists found that they needed their idiosyncratic idiom.

Alice Walker tries to capture the voice of the southern black woman just as Flannery O'Connor, the Roman Catholic writer from Georgia, captures the voice of the poor whites.[53]

Literature will be the richer for this pulling and stretching of language. The neatness is lost, but the liveliness of the speech can be like stepping from the stuffy formal parlor into the fresh air. Once out on her own, the woman has to reach deep within to find the right words to express what she experiences, rather than using standard words for what others think she should experience. She has to discover or to create literary form.

Creating a Market

The artist feels frustrated if she has created space for writing, sought deep in herself for the right words, has painstakingly defined her experience, and then has no opportunity to see print. She needs to be published before the act of communication is complete. She needs readers.

The modern novel is now facing fierce competition from television and film. For the most part, the level of intellect demanded by the visual forms is far beneath the level demanded by the crudest forms of written literature. Even within the literary forms, the violence and explicit sexuality often drive the gentle story with sensitive ideas right out of the marketplace. This is not a new problem. At the beginning of the great era of novel writing, the eighteenth century, Dr. Samuel Johnson registered a parallel complaint about novels. He insisted that his contemporaries had indulged in a level of romantic adventure that was escalating to the point where meditative literature had become unpalatable to the masses.

Actually, subtlety has probably always been lost on the masses. Once the common man and woman became the patrons of the arts—by buying the books and supporting the artists— they became the arbiters of taste. And the average person would prefer lusty adventure to cerebral challenge. Crudeness generally drives sensitivity out of business. If the modern bookstore is any indicator, the range of books on sexual deviation far exceeds any other category. (Perhaps certain limits in television until recently have kept this segment of the book market from well-deserved extinction.)

71

Yet there is always some taste for good writing and for serious ideas, even in the worst of times. The classics continue to sell, and religious bookstores are thriving. Some book publishers have recently initiated "Christian romances," books that applaud modesty and traditional Christian values. Those old favorites—the Bible, *Pilgrim's Progress,* and the works of Dante—continue to hold their place in the modern book market.

Women in search of a publisher need not rush to satisfy the lowest common denominator. They need not be conformed to this world. They can find their voice and speak firmly of their values without blaming a debased world, even if this costs them time and money in the marketplace. Responsible women writers, like responsible men writers, have an obligation to make good use of Christian liberty. We must be transformed and transforming.

chapter five

Woman as Character— Earth Mother to Wonder Woman

Characterizations of women in literature are traced from the ancient Earth Mother creatrix figure through to modern times, including the sainted Mary figure, the tramp, the fallen woman, the single woman, and the modern wonder woman.

Some of the most authentic recent works by women are biographies or autobiographies—works that are shaped like novels but based on fact. When an artist tells her own story, she is more likely to avoid the pitfalls of the modern marketplace. Usually the appetite for self-discovery and communication pushes the artist to tell the truth without an eye to the reader's tastes. She may then catch a character or a culture in the net of art without copying the methods of masculine fiction. Books like *The Bell Jar* or *I Know Why the Caged Bird Sings*, for example, avoid the stereotypical female characters' obvious human relationships and clichéd paths of action. These kinds of books satisfy the woman's new appetite to know more fully other women and the various lives they lead. Having been neatly categorized for centuries, most women cherish their new individualism.

Obviously some biographies are written for the sensationalist market. These may create a character that is more fiction than fact, so ridiculously exaggerated that we sense little shared humanity with the monster portrayed. A book like Jean Stein's *Edie,* for example, describes Edie Sedgwick, a talented and beautiful young woman who was a bright and gifted child of a wealthy New England family.[54] She became a Warhol "superstar," a drug addict, and an anorexic, ruining her promising life by her insatiable appetite for sex and sensation, dying before she discovered how to live. Exposés of Hollywood actresses likewise tend to be formulaic, revealing more sexual than mental activity, producing caricatures rather than characters.

Even autobiographies may commingle fact with fiction to create rather than chronicle. *The Autobiography of Alice B. Toklas,* really the autobiography of Gertrude Stein, is such a creative work.[55] By posing as another person, she is able to describe herself as a genius and attack her enemies. She pretended to be her own best friend and live-in lover, telling of her household in Paris that attracted the talented American writers of the Lost Generation, including F. Scott Fitzgerald and Ernest Hemingway. Stein's work is as eccentric as its author. No one reading the curious prose of Stein could fit her neatly into any stereotypical role for women. She was neither wife nor mother; and "old maid" hardly describes this fierce queen bee.

Another potential layer of truth can be the novel, when used as a thinly veiled biography. The frustration and entrapment that Charlotte Perkins Gilman felt in her brief marriage is vividly portrayed in "The Yellow Wallpaper."[56] *The Bell Jar,* along with her journals, helps us to understand the feelings of Sylvia Plath.[57] Although we may not completely equate the author with the character, we can discover a great deal from the literature that helps us to understand the emotions of the author.

Except for such individualized studies, based on real persons, literature has usually presented women not as individuals, but as types. Woman is rarely the actual *subject* of older literature; she is more commonly the object. Not the woman, but the man is the hero; the woman is the creature for whom the hero seeks or lusts or fights. She may be served or loved or possessed, but she is usually passive. The biographical mode, in contrast, focuses on the active, individual woman—without necessarily being filtered through the male point of view. Occasionally we see an exception to this when the male biographer judges the life of the woman by her ability to conform to male standards for female life. But usually such authors prefer to write about men or women who live lives that reinforce their own values. The female biographer has helped immeasurably in discovering new patterns and individuals, and thereby expanding the perception of female potential.

Selective perception is a universal characteristic. None of us can see everything around us. We select out of the multifarious world those images that fit comfortably in our own intellectual framework. Those unacceptable images that somehow thrust themselves upon us by their enormity or peculiarity or intensity we usually choose to label "aberrations," allowing us to discount them. They do not therefore alter our concept of the norm.

Literature is (among other things) a record of this selective perception, a mirror of this process of organizing life so as to make it comprehensible. It is therefore a useful means of judging the presuppositions of a people. By studying the heroes and heroines, the qualities celebrated and castigated in humans, we can understand something of the cultural norms of the people who produced the literature. We know that Beowulf was a hero to the Anglo-Saxons, even though this mead-drinking underwater wrestler is not our idea of a gentleman. We know that Grendel's mother was no model for Grendel's generation or for ours, even though she was certainly a faithful mother to her monster son. We also know that the Greeks loved the wily Odysseus, but to us he comes across as a liar and a womanizer.

Over the years, the individual cultures change, yet the archetypes hold. We still honor the man of active mind and physical strength. In fact, we rarely depart from an updated Beowulf or Odysseus in our election of a leader. Something of the larger heroic types resonates in us all, regardless of our specific civilization.

In like manner, our image of the female is also set firmly in us. Despite the radical cultural changes we have witnessed in recent years, the archetype perseveres. She need not be Helen of Troy or Cinderella, but we still prefer her over Grendel's mother or one of the ugly stepsisters.

We gravitate toward the woman of exceptional beauty; her intellect is at best secondary. From the ancient hymns to the modern films, any study of Western literature reveals many of the same figures. The following quick survey of these archetypes can help us recognize the assumptions we make. Only by better understanding them can we hope to discover fresh insights.

Ancient Characterizations of Women

The recurrent and overarching female figure is that of the Great Mother—the mythical creatrix who haunts Sumerian and other Near Eastern religions. As discussed in an earlier chapter, she reverberates through Greek and Roman religions and continues to be revived from time to time as a matriarchal symbol. Currently she serves those who dispute the patriarchal cast of the Judeo-Christian tradition. For example, a contemporary poster that appeals to both feminists and environmentalists pictures the earth with a legend that reads, "Love thy mother."[58] This Mother Goddess is a colorful figure, a kind of Mother Earth. In some of the ancient myths she is thought to have been impregnated by a snake and to have laid the universal egg from which all life comes. In some ways she is a facet of Eve—the mother of all living. In other stories she was thought to have been cut in two like a mollusk to form the heavens and the earth. Sexual creation myths naturally abound among primitive folk; after all, sexual creation was immediately comprehensible.

Early art reveals an abundance of fertility cult figures, often images that were buried in the ground to encourage the harvest. As a rule they appear to be all belly and breasts, with almost no face or capacity for action (i.e., no hands or feet). The worship of this figure under the guise of Ishtar, Astarte, or Diana (as noted earlier) was widespread. In Sumerian myth she was the goddess of both love and war—the symbol of the womb and of the tomb, of birth and of death.

Woman, long cherished for her fertility, still is so regarded today. The traditional curse in biblical culture was the curse of the barren womb. Rarely were unmarried or childless women admired. The ideal woman was fecund. After all, the large family was the symbol of the man's virility, of God's blessing. When Job was cursed, he lost all of his children. When he was blessed, he had a whole new tribe of them. For the ancient man an abundance of children was the assurance that his "seed" would continue after him, providing a kind of physical afterlife. We know that this fertility goddess lured the Israelites into acts of pagan worship. The groves of Astarte were the places where Jezebel worshiped. And we know from subsequent references that Jezebel was not alone in the groves of Ishtar. The prophet Hosea describes his wife Gomer in ways that suggest she was a prostitute of Ishtar.[59] Women who worshiped at her shrine were expected, as an act of piety, to give themselves to the first man who approached them. Sexual service, the appropriate act of worship for temple prostitutes, was common in numerous cities of the Greek and Roman world.

Nor has the fertility goddess disappeared from our experience with the years. We may call her Aphrodite or Venus or Marilyn or Liz, but she still remains the voluptuous image of sexual fulfillment—an image by and for men. The angle of vision is enthusiastically masculine. Women who worship at her shrine think of themselves as they relate to men—mistresses or mothers or wives. They dream of themselves as human equivalents of the Great Goddess, impressive in their fecundity, dedicated to the service of sexuality. The more we contemplate the multiple apparitions of this Mother Goddess, the more facets of her we perceive.

Literary Images of the Mother Goddess

Most men know women in two major roles—as mother and as wife (or lover). In literature sisters and friends are less common images—unless a sister or a friend should become a temptress to the young man.

For the boy child, nursing at his mother's ample breast and later running to her for comfort or protection, the mother is the very image of security. As the child grows up and joins the world of men, he still remembers the embraces of the mother. In his wanderings and adventures, he may develop such a sentiment for her that she becomes the embodiment of everything good in childhood. Her image is home. Her mood is peace. Her talent is healing. Erich Neumann (in his impressive book *The Great Mother*) calls her "the nurturing mother."[60]

In other stories this mother is not so perfect. Rather than nurture the child and then push him out of the nest, she refuses to let him go. She uses that love to smother him. The umbilical cord becomes the psychological bond that fixes the young man to her. Instead of serving as home for the eternal wanderer, she turns the image into a loving prison. By her hovering love, she emasculates and cripples him.

This monster figure is the devouring mother. In ancient myth she is often an old monster who tricks the hero and tries to disable him. She can be a Medusa with snakes for hair or a Harpy with wings and a sharp beak or a Medea with witchcraft that allows her to turn a wedding dress into a blanket of fire, stripping the charred flesh right off the bones. This dragon lady is usually older than the hero and always ruthless in her attacks. In fairy tales she is the wicked stepmother who envys the beauty of the heroine and seeks her death or misfortune.[61]

Once the hero breaks loose from the good or evil mother, he faces the other archetypes—those of the beloved. If she should be a young idealist, full of goodness and light, leading him to heroism and to heights of fulfillment, she is the saintly figure—Sophia. Such a lady of dreams is less common in ancient literature than in medieval. The ancients were more inclined to believe this woman who drove man to adventure to be the wife or the goddess. Pallas Athena loved men who risked their lives in her service. At the end of *The Odyssey,* we realize that Odysseus, with Athena's help, has made his strenuous efforts to return to his wife and child. They become his guiding stars.

Alas, not all women lure men to do good. Some lovely faces cover sinister souls. The alluring sirens sang beautifully, but the sailors who listened to their songs soon wrecked on the rocks. The Germans had the Rhinemaidens, their own ladies of the rocks, who enchanted men and destroyed them. This evil temptress is the classic villain of literature—the hussy or the tramp who confuses the naïve youth and sends him off on the path to perdition.

Each of these four women—the good mother and the bad mother, the good lover and the bad lover—is judged by her treatment of the male. She has no real life outside of her relationship to him. And usually there is no effort to judge his actions toward her. She is a relation, an object, a part of the story—always adjunct, never the main event. She may be the wife of Jacob or the mother of Joseph or the temptation of David but not an individual with her very own history. It is no wonder that the greatest dream possible for ancient woman was to be wife or mother to the hero.

The sirens or Medusa or the Harpies are all part of stories about Odysseus or Jason. Rarely does an author suggest that a Medea is not just a seductress and sinister mother, capable of killing her own children and murdering Jason's new lover. Euripides is remarkable for understanding that this monster mother is also a cruelly mistreated woman with anger and hurts and needs. His tragic masterpiece, *Medea,* is a remarkable example of changing the focus from the hero to the woman who first saves and then destroys his life.[62] Aeschylus and Sophocles also drew strong women. Clytemnestra and Electra and Antigone are characters who refuse to be mother/wife images.[63] They live as vivid individuals. Whatever the social role of women in Greek culture, strong individuals must have broken out of those roles to serve as models for such powerful characters.

Mary as Myth

Needless to say, the primal mother figure did not disappear with the fall of Athens. While city-states and kingdoms rose and fell, she retained her enduring power. By the Middle Ages she reappeared as the Virgin Mary. The simple Hebrew maiden of the Gospels was gradually credited with much of the magical power of the Mother Goddess.

Some believe that Mary spent her final years in Ephesus with the apostle John. It was in Ephesus, interestingly enough, in that ancient city where the cultures of the East and of the West met, that Paul had his conflict with the worshipers of Diana. The silversmiths resented Christendom's attack on Diana, the local version of the Mother Goddess. (Primitive peoples are less likely to abandon their nature worship than to transfer it.) Yet Mary is no simple fertility symbol. She existed in the flesh as a real person with her own story to tell. For the Jew she was a symbol of Hebrew woman's dream to mother forth the Messiah. For the Christian she was an example of redeemed humanity, choosing subjection and service to God, and thereby achieving glory. As

the virgin mother, she combined the purity of the Sophia figure
and the creativity of the Good Mother. Medieval man thought
she could lead him to salvation. Her life became the classic path
for the saint—the way to perfect Christian womanhood. Gradually church tradition has expanded her history so that hers too
was a virgin birth and she too ended earthly life with an
assumption. The medieval paintings of her show her as the
Queen of Heaven, enthroned with the child on her lap and later
at her breast, while angels gather around like royal courtiers. The
moon—Diana's sign of fertility—is still part of her iconography.
Motherhood is still her essence.

Medieval scholars note that Mariolatry altered many of
Western culture's attitudes toward women and thereby changed
the role of women in literature.[64] In the medieval romances, for
example, women became virginal figures, enthroned and adored
by knights who would serve them as figures of the greater saint—
Mary. Stories of King Arthur's knights show a veneration for
women that verges on idolatry. The Provençal writers also
fostered this romantic adoration. Knights would wear their
ladies' sleeves into battle, dedicating their lives to the service of
their beloved. These relations seldom served as a courtship in
our sense. They were not necessarily a prelude to marriage, nor
were they necessarily hindered by the woman's marriage to
another man.

When Dante in the *Divine Comedy* begins his descent into Hell
and his ascent into Purgatory and Heaven, he seeks the guidance
of his lady, Beatrice. On the trip he is aided by this woman, now
living in Paradise. Although never married to her, he adored
from afar her goodness and beauty while she was alive. She
sends other ladies to lead him along the way, and her love
encourages him to keep seeking the good path. It is through the
love of Beatrice that Dante can rise to the love of goodness, and
of beauty, and of the Virgin, and of Christ, and of God—a kind
of ladder of love.

The Lady and the Tramp

Among the more curious effects of this elevation of the Virgin
Mary, then, is the alteration of the mother figure into an
unattainable lady love, a Sophia. She becomes the lady on the

pedestal who calls men forth to noble action, but does not deign to satisfy their ignoble lust. This idealization of the lady is balanced by the denigration of the slut. The figures of lust are increasingly seen as forbidden and nasty—temptresses and whores. Sexuality is despised as a sign of the flesh and of human weakness.

The temptress is one of the oldest images of woman. In Hebrew interpretation of Scripture, we have Eve handing the apple to Adam and thereby causing him to fall from innocence. (The Greeks had a parallel story of Pandora, who opened up the forbidden box and let all of the world's ills fly out.)

Later biblical women were man-traps in a somewhat less cosmic manner. David, when he was king of Israel, saw Bathsheba taking a bath on her rooftop, invited her over, and finally ordered the murder of her husband. She could not help being beautiful and probably could not have refused the advances of a king. But she and David were to suffer the death of their child as punishment for their sin.

Other women—like Helen of Troy—also proved breeders of conflict because of their beauty. Lusty Paris came to Sparta, took Helen and the silver, and ran back to Troy. The result was the Trojan War. But Homer and his culture seem to have viewed Helen as a pawn in a man's game, not to blame for the abduction or the war. After all was done and Troy was in ashes, she went back to Sparta for a genteel old age.

Other great beauties were more specifically at fault. Delilah tempted Samson, cut off his hair, and brought on his tragedy. Jezebel enticed her husband to steal and kill. Later when she was thrown from her window and eaten by dogs, we are led to believe that she deserved her hideous death.

The problem is not beauty but its misuse: as a temptation for man to act wrongly. If a young woman such as Esther uses her beauty to save her people, her temptation is good. If she uses it against God, as does Delilah, her temptation is evil.

Today the temptress persists in our literature—the cynical call girl, the fortune hunter, the devious exploiter of innocent man, and the destroyer of families. One of the best examples in the nineteenth century was Becky Sharp, a main character in *Vanity Fair* who proved far more interesting than her innocent counterpart.[65] The current metamorphosis of this temptress figure has

expanded our understanding of her motives and frustrations.
Declining moral values and increasing psychological and sociological justification have neutralized her. Without a sense of sin,
she cannot be a sinner. After all, if she has no way to achieve her
will except by luring men to act on her behalf, she must use those
handy weapons of beauty and sensuality. Her cynicism, critics
insist, is motivated by a repressive society of which she is a part.
Even the word *slut* is disappearing, and the world instead views
such a woman as a "happy hooker." Obviously Scripture
preserves moral distinctions (as do Christians). (The judgment
falls on the sin, not the sinner.) But she must go and sin no more,
not find happiness in her sin. While the Christian reader need not
insist on simplistic good and evil, neither need she accept evil as
inevitable.

Fallen Woman

The character of the bad girl is always colorful. Evil invariably
seems more fascinating than good. The judgments of good and
evil are themselves mirrors of the values of our society. For
example, a girl is seen as "fallen" if she has slept with someone
before marriage. On the other hand, the Fall is much more
impressive. It involves the whole temptation in the Garden of
Eden, the desire to know more than God wanted humans to
know, the rebellion and refusal to serve their Maker. The fall of
woman is merely physical—the illicit breaking of the hymen.

This is not the way Genesis portrays the same scene. Woman's
fall, like man's, is the rebellion against God. A fallen woman is
one who no longer lives in primal innocence, who has known the
taste of forbidden fruit. Surely sexual indulgence is not the only
form of sin known to woman. To isolate this as the single
indicator of the good and evil in woman is a denial of woman's
total humanity.

In the famous eighteenth-century novel *The Vicar of Wakefield*
by Oliver Goldsmith, a lovely young woman is tricked into a
bogus marriage.[66] She finds that she has been sleeping with a
man to whom she is not legally married. She then returns home
in shame. Her song summarizes her tragedy and reflects the
mind-set of the era:

> When lovely woman stoops to folly,
> And finds too late that men betray,
> What charm can soothe her melancholy,
> What art can wash her guilt away?

The song ends with advice that the heroine herself accepts. To compensate for her evil acts and to show her lover the error of his ways, she must die:

> The only art her guilt to cover,
> To hide her shame from every eye,
> To give repentance to her lover,
> And wring his bosom—is, to die.

In real life a fair number of women have seen an illegitimate pregnancy (now called a "problem pregnancy") as the reason for suicide, but surely none of us believes that this is a good solution. The real problem is to find a way to live past pain and disappointment into a new life, discovering meaning through evil. The Christian reader surely believes that sin can be forgiven and one can have redemption and continue with life. Despair is the unforgivable sin.

Hardy's *Tess of the d'Urbervilles* offers a similar story. Again the girl is taken against her will and finds herself forever labeled as "bad." Clearly one of the problems of being on the pedestal is that it is so easy to fall off. And once fallen, women lie forever in the gutter. The Christian would never accept this elevated notion of human nature in the first place. If one believes that the human being is born in sin, then no pedestals are available for either men or women. And with the acceptance of our fallen state also comes the understanding of our tendency to sin. Recognition of this nature allows us to forgive more easily because we see our own need to be forgiven.

The world at large, operating on the Romantic concept of human beings' inherent goodness, is always shocked by evil. The exaggerated notion of human potential allows for no error and then for no forgiveness, and no chance for redemption or reform. A recent Broadway show illustrates this point. *Agnes of God*[67] is the story of a saintly nun who bears and kills a child. At one moment she sees herself as totally depraved and unforgivable. At the next she denies any memory of her evil acts and strives to be a stained-glass saint. Incapable of accepting her hopelessly mixed nature and her responsibility for an act of lust and violence, she cannot deal with her sins. She cannot accept her common humanity and therefore cannot find the path to salvation. Seeking to be a saint without God's help or forgiveness, she ends in madness and self-destruction.

A contrary literary example appears in T. S. Eliot's "Wasteland."[68] The poem portrays men and women as uniformly nasty. His arid world has neither innocence, nor guidelines for recognizing good and evil, nor hope for cleansing and redemption. The poem chronicles some of the cynical attitudes current in the years following World War I. The lovely lady in this poem stoops to folly and learns that men betray (if betrayal is possible in a world without values or commitment). The weary typist, home from the office, accepts the squalid advances of the carbuncular clerk, expecting no love nor romance nor permanence. He couples with her in the twilight moment of lust and then leaves. Rather than lament her fall or commit suicide, she puts another record on the Gramophone. The world (Eliot suggested even before his own conversion) has turned from too sacred a view of chastity to too profane a view. Now sex means less than a handshake.

This is certainly true in most novels and plays that have followed World War II. Often the characters sleep together before they exchange names and addresses. An intermediate position appears in the classic study of adultery, *The Scarlet Letter,* by Nathaniel Hawthorne. Here the woman works her way through the sin of fornication to her punishment and redemption, while the man remains forever fallen. One acknowledges her sin and turns the fruits into the basis for a new life; the other hides his and turns the denial into a living death.

The nineteenth century was replete with stories of violated women. The romantics' pure woman furnished the satanic Byronic hero with a perfect victim. Don Juans delighted the audience by despoiling angelic heroines by the dozen. Gothic novels are especially colorful in their use of lily-white maidens about to be despoiled by ruthless satyrs. The evil men are melodramatic villains twirling their mustachios as they leer at the lovely maidens. This shadow of the Marquis de Sade still lurks about, the sinister figure in Gothic murder mysteries. A special kind of titillation appears to result from the defloration of the beautiful blonde maiden. (Blondes, it would seem, are more fragile and innocent than brunettes.) The whole pattern suggests the world's insatiable appetite for perversity.

The Wicked Woman

The romantic evil lady, the sinister brunette, is the lineal descendant of our Lady of the Rocks. She is the siren in Victorian dress. As Lamia or *la belle dame sans merci*,[69] she is the vampire or snake figure, the blood sucker. In contemporary films this is the James Bond woman, a vixen with no morals or inhibitions. Usually exotically beautiful, she is the modern witch. This Venus flytrap lures the innocent worshiper with her exotic and poisonous scents. In Keats' "Lamia" and Coleridge's "Christabel" she is the enemy of man.[70]

For the realistic novel neither the blonde victim nor the brunette vixen is especially useful. Both are too clearly caricatures of experience. Life is seldom so clearly good or evil as to allow us to know such unmitigated examples in the flesh. Nor is symbolism much help in sorting out our judgments. In fact, some blondes are no better than they have to be, and some brunettes may turn out all right in the end. But the popular imagination continues to cherish the medieval dream symbols of the saint and the gargoyle. Part of the experience of youthful romance is to reduce the other person to a creature of other-worldly attributes, for whom the poet will sing and the warrior will die. Gatsby's dream girl is worth a lifetime of winning.[71] She stays ideal because she is never won. Like the nymph on the Grecian urn, she is always beautiful and always out of reach.[72]

The Good Love and the Bad One

The wife herself, the woman won and known, is rarely central to traditional fiction. The patient wife is a valuable example. The unfaithful or deceitful one is valuable as a warning. Ancient aristocratic men saw women as possessions to be bought and sold.

The Christian era brought some changes in the status of woman, but progress has been spotty at best. Even lacking equal rights, women frequently found life bearable through the ages.

Up until the nineteenth century, women clearly had a number of useful functions in the household, and their work kept them busy—and sometimes content. In fact, many homes were small industrial centers where weaving and spinning and baking and brewing and sewing were all managed by the wife. But the preference of the middle class for conspicuous waste encouraged women to relinquish their chores to industries outside of the home and dedicate their days to calling on one another, embroidering samplers, and reading novels. Aping their aristocratic forebears, aspiring Victorian men cherished the opulence of this status symbol—the ornamental and useless wife.

The modern woman bears the imprint of her sex's history. Like her Victorian sisters, the "good wife and mother" is faithful to her husband, conscientious about her household, and sacrificial with her children. Her primary concern is their health and convenience and happiness. Her middle-class prejudice may discourage this homemaker or "domestic engineer" from entering the job market. Or, if she should take work for pay, she tends to apologize for taking the job, for fear it is a commentary on her husband's ability to earn a decent living. Lower-class women have always had to work outside of the house—in fields or in factories. When money was needed for the household, wives in most countries have traditionally been a significant part of the work force. They never needed to seek excuses for their labor.

At the other extreme, wives of the upper classes were always free to move around beyond the confines of onerous household labors. Aristocrats were the first women to be educated and to venture into literature. (So it is the wives of the middle class who have the problem of appropriate position.) Dorothy L. Sayers claimed that most of the meaningful and entertaining work has moved out of the household. Thus women, increasingly educated like men, increasingly independent financially like men, increasingly also want to have flexible lives—like men. No man is forced to choose between career and marriage (unless he is the king of England and has chosen an unsuitable mate). Women often wonder why they must.

Modern novels then have begun to focus on the woman after marriage, when she is older and faced with problems other than attracting or fending off lusty men. While the classic male novel has been the man's coming of age, the modern female novel may turn out to be the middle-age (or the mid-life) crisis. This is the point in the woman's life when she must decide among her multiple roles and thereby come to a definition of herself.

An early example of this break in the Victorian housewife tradition is Kate Chopin's book *The Awakening*.[73] Recently discovered by feminist critics, the novel is a classic description of housewifely discontent. Set in nineteenth-century Louisiana, this is the story of a pampered, languid, dissatisfied, and purposeless woman. Lovely children and generous husband are not enough to content this woman who has other vaguely artistic needs. She tries romance, separation, painting, and swimming. None of them really works. Seeing no hope and no possibility for return to her earlier contentment with her sheltered lot, she finally walks into the Gulf and drowns.

If we consider *The Awakening* from the point of view of people trying to live meaningful lives, we must wonder whether the heroine had to leave home, whether the new sexual liaison was essential, and whether suicide was the inevitable conclusion. All of these are dramatic activities that involve the reader, but all are simplistic and suspect when applied to real life. The heroine's total dedication to self hardly deserves our respect.

Finding a way to live is a tougher and far more rewarding path than finding a way to die. We must be cautious in applauding the heroine who elects this violent exit. (I recall a student who thought Hedda Gabler was heroic to commit suicide. She herself committed suicide shortly after that.) As Christian thinkers, we do not want anyone to believe that we really approve the choices that literature provides as extreme examples.

A more positive response than Chopin's would be to find a way to grow and mature and to find one's own proper work. If possible, this should be within the commitments already made and deserving of being honored, but at the very least it should be within rational limits. We must not assume that every housewife is unhappy, or that every unhappy woman is a frustrated artist of incredible genius. Some people, both men and women, just want more adventure or more love or more money. All discontent is not necessarily divine.

Art, by its very nature, works with extreme cases and stark images, as some of the examples cited illustrate. Slamming the door is a far more dramatic literary device than charting the labyrinthine conversation that leads to the temporary solution. Immature women need to consider education and work, not simply romantic escape. When dreamy romanticism has gone out of a marriage, the hero or the heroine may look about for a new partner. Rather than step across the threshold in a mature phase of love, they retreat into the adolescent thrill of forbidden sex. Readers clearly enjoy such stories, partially as vicarious adventure. Certainly this temptation is not peculiar to fiction, as the current divorce rate suggests. Novelists and film makers are inclined to celebrate youth and romance and freedom rather than maturity and love and fidelity.

If the novel purports to be realistic, we need to apply realistic criteria in judging it: youth is fleeting, education takes effort, work is not glamorous, and freedom can be as boring as frustration.

As times change, the images change. Although the good housewife fighting waxy buildup lingers in the magazine ads, she is becoming rare in significant literature. The "little woman" who stands as a helpmeet behind her superachieving husband is also disappearing. In her place the articulate partner has emerged, who asks the same questions as her husband, who shares many of his drives, and who faces many of the same temptations. The subsequent emergence of the man-as-mother in modern films is interesting as a reminder that roles may even be reversed. Some men would prefer to be "househusbands," and some women are happy as financial wizards.

The Single Woman

Modern literature has one fresh new character—the older single woman. She rarely appears in ancient literature. The solitary woman apparently was an anomaly in polygamous societies. Her father would simply give her as an additional wife to a friend or sell her as a bondswoman to a stranger. The terms of such trades form a large part of Mosaic Law. Few single women—other than widows—appear in the Old Testament. Miriam, we assume, was such a person. She cared for her brothers, Moses and Aaron, and Scripture notes no husband or children for her. Miriam chanted her victory song for the escape of the Israelites from Egypt, led the women in singing and dancing, and later prophesied. She was recognized as a leader in Israel (see Mic. 6:4), but she apparently instigated Aaron to join her in challenging Moses' leadership. This action put her in conflict with the Lord because He had chosen Moses as the leader over all Israel. God then punished her with leprosy (for one week).[74]

In ancient Greek literature the unmarried woman also proved difficult. Antigone caused a lot of trouble because she was not willing to obey the laws of the men around her. Electra encouraged her brother to murder their mother. Both were obedient to gods rather than to men. And the maenads[75] were maidens who ran in frenzy through the forests, seeking men and animals to dismember in bloody rituals of worship. The Greeks, it would seem, believed that women need the authority of a good strong male to keep them sane and satisfied. But the writers do honor them for their idealism and their tragic intensity about values.

The New Testament message is quite different. Jesus made friends with two single sisters, Mary and Martha. They appear to have been in charge of the household where Lazarus their brother also lived, perhaps indicating that Martha was a widow. At any rate, these were not mad women nor were they rebels against the state. They sat with Jesus to discuss theology in a thoughtful and sensible manner.

Mary Magdalene is another interesting example of Jesus' friendship with a single woman. In fiction Mary Magdalene would have been the love interest, either the pure maiden who inspires the hero to do his work or the impure temptress who lures him to his perdition.[76] Instead Mary was a friend and disciple. Medieval artists often characterize her as a red-haired sinner, kneeling on one side of the cross, in balanced contrast with the blue-clad Virgin Mary. Scripture records nothing to suggest that Jesus saw Mary Magdalene or any other woman as "fallen" in some special sense (i.e., any more "fallen" than men). Even the woman taken in adultery had no accusers, not even the perfect Son of God. The Gospel narratives record that Mary Magdalene, like the mother of Jesus, was among the last at the cross and the first at the tomb. She was also among the disciples waiting for the Holy Spirit in the Upper Room.

Single women, except for the saint or the maiden, are rarely characters in literature until after the Middle Ages. They may not have been so visible until that time. Although women are born in larger numbers than men, wars tend to kill off men in larger numbers than women. So long as there were large households, women could stay with their brothers or their fathers as part of a supernumerary family. The Christian insistence on monogamy had brought to a halt the old custom of multiple wives. And the church did not encourage the believers to sell off their daughters. For a time, convents became an acceptable alternative to marriage for Christian women. But in England the closing of the convents at the time of the Reformation blocked this path for unmarried women.

In Protestant England the women in the households were often seen as little more than upper servants. Milton's daughters are frequently cited as women drafted unwillingly into service of their dominating father. By the eighteenth century, such women were becoming better educated and more independent. The only artistic careers open, however, were the unladylike ones of writing or performing on the stage. Lower-middle-class women could earn a subsistence as governesses. If the nineteenth-century novels are to be believed, these jobs were thoroughly demeaning. An isolated woman without wealth or position was neither servant nor family and consequently very vulnerable. Jane Austen and the Brontës portrayed such women as educated slaves. No wonder women would prefer to marry any kind of man. At least as matrons they then had some social standing.

The nineteenth century saw the emergence of the single woman as a powerful social and political force. Some of these ladies discovered that they could retain control over their property only if they remained single. In England until the Married Women's Property Act, any married woman lost to the husband all claim to her property and to any earnings she might have in the future.[77] Propertied single women organized movements for prohibition, abolition, and women's suffrage. The nineteenth century is full of women's manifestoes, women's economic theories, women's political speeches, women's sermons, women's revision of Scripture, women's political lobbies, and other public activities for and by women. The vastly improved life for twentieth-century women is the direct result of the efforts of nineteenth-century women who lobbied vigorously to open colleges to women, to open careers to women, to open suffrage to women, and to give women equal rights.

The historical changes brought commensurate changes in the literary characterization of the single woman. Too old to be the heroine, too plain to be the beloved, she at first became the caricature of the old maid—the spinster. Sometimes she was the troublemaker and gossip, sometimes a preacher and a rabble-rouser. Then gradually she became a sojourner seeking truth. She had evolved from antiheroine to hero.

An interesting early modern example of this unmarried woman is Edith Wharton's Lily Bart.[78] This bright, independent woman cannot find her place in "the house of mirth." She keeps looking for a spot in life that will allow her to use her talents and satisfy her appetite for meaning. She finds that the culture has no place for her. Cast aside, unable to conform or transform, she dies. A later heroine, like Ellen Glasgow's strong woman in *Barren Ground,* turns from a dependent ruined woman to a strong independent woman, able to live with or without men. The figure is not necessarily beautiful; she may, in fact, be rather too masculine for popular taste. But heroines through the ages have been noted for their toughness rather than for their beauty. This appears to be the price for assuming the new role. The Christian critic need not seek to force a return to the status quo. She needs rather to judge the ethical stance of this new creation, combining fresh insights and undying verities.

Wonder Woman

In modern films the new woman is portrayed as the jogger with a career, able to fend for herself in a tough world. She can be a Diana or a Deborah or a Joan of Arc, but she may also be a businesswoman or a professor or a scientist. She can drive a car or a truck, toss a man over her shoulder, and (if she should decide to have a family) love the kids without hovering over them. She may prefer the company of women to that of men; she is not afraid of close women friends. Nor is she afraid of sexual encounters. They may or may not mean a lot to her. She has all the independence of the old male hero of the Hemingway story. We have seen her on TV as a policewoman or the corporate executive. We should expect to see her more and more in novels as she now appears with increasing frequency in life.

We may not approve of her, but we must acknowledge that she is no wimp. An egocentric female is no more heroic than an egocentric male. We have created dubious models in an effort to conform to masculine (and pagan) value systems. Now, at last, authors may allow her to show some Christian charity and morality.

We have come a long way from the Earth Mother to the androgynous Wonder Woman, but this is not to say that the old Earth Mother has disappeared. Heroes and heroines still run back to their mother or mammy, depending on whether she is white or black. Nurturing mother figures still form an intrinsic part of life and of art. Nor has the fragile heroine of the medieval romance fluttered off into oblivion. Romances are still full of pure young innocents, threatened by lust-crazed villains, and saved by handsome young adorers. Novels still most often end with marriage, as if that were the climax of the woman's life or of the man's adventures.

But modern novelists are increasingly inclined to see women as individuals who have choices to make that are every bit as complex as men's choices. The pattern is inclining toward an existential view of woman. She is defining herself daily as she makes her decisions. Not uniformly good or evil, not just a mother or a temptress or a witch, woman has reality of her own. All our images and judgments of them need not be male-oriented and clumsy. Women need not be tangential to men or restricted to masculine relationships.

A woman, says Simone de Beauvoir, is considered a creature of immanence. A man, by contrast, is transcendent. Thus, a woman traditionally brackets the life of man and forms the anchor for his life. But he is the one who thrusts out into space, taking risks, having adventures, and then finally returning home to woman. She is there at his birth. She nurtures his seed, assuring his immortality, his children. She mourns his death. The *Madonna* and the *Pieta* are classic portrayals of women in traditional roles. The Sophia or siren are all corollary to man. But the man is stage-center.

The time is now at hand when both sexes will be portrayed in literature as free individuals, truly liberated, eager to discover the values that make life an adventure not limited to men only or to youth only or to marriage. Stories can be full of middle-aged women with sagging breasts and thick glasses, some of whom are engineers and some teachers and some mothers. They may or may not have men in their lives, and men are not the entire *raison d'être* for those lives. Women characters can be as varied and colorful as men, now that women's lives are becoming as varied and colorful as men's.

For the time being, contrary or compensatory stereotypes are arising. The Wonder Woman syndrome tends to emasculate all of the male characters. New businesswomen may be as foolish as Babbitt, and the new liberated singles may be Donna Juanitas. Those few female characters who do want to stay at home to tend large families and cook gourmet meals are pictured as ridiculous anachronisms. Gentle women who love children are pictured as doormats and mindless mates. This is patently unfair.

But every age, every new development, has followed a similar path. The pendulum always swings too far. A time of compensation and destruction usually precedes a time of rebuilding and freedom. An infantile destructiveness seems to signal the process of breaking free. Real freedom comes when we are no longer controlled by old stereotypes—or at least when we no longer uncritically accept them as our own presuppositions. At that moment we shall be truly liberated and so will our literature.

chapter six

The Shape of Life

The author discusses the three stages of life described for women in ancient literature: the maiden, the wife, and the crone. She demonstrates how writing about women's concerns can revolutionize the shape of values presented in literature.

So what happened? Once we have the characters and the words to describe the events, we want to know what happened. What is the story?

One episode of the popular TV sit-com "All in the Family" showed the twenty-fifth class reunion at Edith Bunker's high school. A friend spotted Edith, gave her a hug, and said, "What have you been doing all these years?" Always literal in her response, Edith drew a deep breath and then launched into her interminable narration, starting with the day of graduation and plodding through each event that she could recall, with no effort to select the memorable from the forgettable. Her old friend was soon fighting to stay awake.

Life and Order—The Nature of Literary Form

Putting incidents into significant order is the art of narration. Selecting out of the enormous multiplicity of events and ideas in all of human life a single line of action, a cluster of characters and events, and arranging these for clarity, suspense, and meaning—these are the chores of the storyteller. While poetry is shaped by formal constraints—length, rhyme, and meter—prose tends to be far more open.

There is really no significant difference between the shape of poetry written by males and that written by females. A poem may or may not have a story. It may simply present an image, a scene, an emotion, or an insight. It need not have a plot, though it will have a form or a shape, and that form (if it is a good poem) will mirror the content perfectly. The message of love or violence or frustration will find an appropriate rhythm, which balances or exaggerates the wild or controlled passions. Each poetic genre has its own expectations that strike the writer as appropriate for the idea or emotion she seeks to communicate. A modern poet like Sylvia Plath chooses the free form of modern poetry and the violent speech of personal outrage to vent her love/hate for "Daddy."[79] Others have chosen the chiseled shape of the sonnet to sing of love or the gentle rhymes of the lyric to express their emotions.

For the most part, women have been best known for lyrical poetry. Christina Rossetti, Elizabeth Barrett Browning, and Emily Dickinson have long claimed the public's respect for their works. They have had less impact on form, however, than have the novelists. With poetry, a multiplicity of forms is already in place. The role of the artist is to select and to alter as she can. With prose, the forms are more varied and less sanctified, and therefore far more malleable.

Novels more clearly bear the imprint of their maker, largely because the form has fewer formal preconceptions than poetry. In fact, literary critics have some difficulty in establishing a definition of the form. A novel can be as poetic as free verse, as obscene as graffiti, as long as an epic, or as short as an anecdote. It can be contemporary or historical, comic or tragic, polemic or philosophic. The plot may follow a neat narrative line to a climax or it may fall to a tragic catastrophe or it may circle back on itself or it may gallop along from one episode to another. Some conventions have developed through usage, but none bears the weight of classical authority. Henry Fielding, an eighteenth-century novelist, tried to make us believe that the novel is a comic epic in prose, but his theory had as many opponents as defenders.[80]

Novels are, in fact, often categorized not by form, but by subject matter—historical or Gothic or adventure or pedagogical or psychological. The subject will, in turn, determine much of its own proper form, whether chronological or stream-of-consciousness or flashbacks or dream sequences. An epistolary form, for example, can be a good device for capturing the excitement of the moment and allowing various characters to explain their motives and ideas from individual perspectives. Meditative flashbacks and time overlays may serve better to provide evocative and philosophic considerations of youth by older heroines.

A thoughtful and sensitive artist has numerous choices to make: does this demand an outburst of passionate feeling (more appropriate to a poem) or an extended discussion (more fitted to an essay) or a fictional narration at some length (a short story or a novel)? If the extended form seems appropriate, then she must decide on the characters, the setting (time and place), the mood, the point of view, the general tone, the theme, and the level of diction. Most of these fall naturally into place as the work grows.

The writer is free to choose the ideas or experiences or images that demand expression and develop a work that is appropriate for that content. She is limited primarily by her own talent, training, and experience, her need to please a publisher, and her audience's formal expectations. As a consequence, women's novels usually mirror the concerns and formal designs of their male counterparts.

For example, Jane Austen, a self-conscious and careful artist, contrasts dramatically with Charles Dickens. While he wrote stories of young men coming of age, she wrote *Emma,* a novel about a young woman entering the mature world. Male authors, with their pedagogical novels or bildungsromans, preferred to portray the adolescent male crossing the threshold of maturity. He escaped from home, wandered among threatening peoples, met and succumbed to the temptations of wicked women and evil men, discovered true love, and eventually returned home to love and fortune and maturity. This is the rite of the man's coming of age. It is an old, old story, echoing the adventures of Joseph or Achilles or Jason or David. Making the hero a contemporary middle-class Englishman does not really alter the epic or the romance.

Coming of age for women has been quite a different story. Women are less likely to mark that moment by a geographical change—except by moving from one home to another in the same village. Certainly Austen's Emma could not leave home— even after she came of age.

Emma was a lovely, if headstrong, young woman who had never been far from her father's house or from the town of her birth. Her small cluster of friends exchanged visits or gossip. Her most wrenching experience was her dear governess's marriage and departure. This was hardly a life replete with adventure. Jane Austen sent her on a picnic or a visit to her neighbors, provided her with temptations of flirting with a newcomer or speaking impetuously. Though the emotions are intense, the physical adventure is constrained and internalized. Colorful scenes are left unexpressed in this civilized culture. Repression and exaggerated attention to detail replace a gallop in the country and a roll in the hay.

What marks the coming of age for most women in most cultures? Is Austen right? Is it simply the need to select a mate? For women is this the grand adventure?

Biology is a more tyrannical force in the woman's life than in the man's. For the young woman the physical coming of age is the shocking recognition of her femaleness, of her ability to bear children. The periodic flow of blood, so closely allied to the phases of the moon, reminds the girl child that she is now potentially a mother, that childhood is past. This initiates a pattern of oneness with the adult female community. The wise old women of the culture must tell her what the discharge means, how to cleanse herself, how to deal with this "curse," and how to protect herself. She is now prepared to migrate from the old family to the new one that will be headed by her husband. Her father removes the risk of incest from his house by "giving" her in marriage to the new man, who initiates her into the mysteries of fertility. Traditionally she does not break away. She is released or stolen.

This is all very well for primitive peoples who discuss such topics as blood and pregnancy. But in Jane Austen's world, babies suddenly appear without any reference to menstruation, sex, or pregnancy. If Emma has discovered what causes babies, she never shares the knowledge with us. Even when Emma decides to marry a man whom she has known all of her life, she slips her hand through her lover's arm, and they walk through the garden. Jane Austen is too much of a lady—or too ignorant of the game of love—to describe the love scene, which by all rights should form the climax of the story.

And as for leaving her father, heaven forbid! She expects her husband to move into the house and help her keep the old man company. Only death will separate her from her father.

The maturing process for Emma is less sexual than moral, psychological, and emotional. Threatened with the loss of the man she loves, she discovers her own flaws and foolishness. Her great adventure had been in tinkering with other people's lives and feelings. Her coming home is her recognition of herself.

The book is uneventful by most standards. The politeness and circumspection cover the limited but intensely felt lives of middle-class women in the nineteenth century. She has selected those materials from her life that alter the form, concentrating it and intensifying it and forcing us to read it differently from the way we would read Dickens' *Great Expectations* or Fielding's *Tom Jones*. By her gentle irony and precise phrasing and balancing of scenes, she has mirrored life and changed the shape of the novel.

Another example of choices and resulting shapes comes from late nineteenth-century America. By the end of the century, Theodore Dreiser, Frank Norris, and others were writing about mature businessmen who were fighting their own dragons to achieve success, while more romantic (or naturalistic) authors like Stephen Crane wrote about other mature men fighting the hostile elements.[81] They were all following a path explored much earlier by Homer, who saw Odysseus meeting challenges along his path back to Ithaca. For the mature man the security of his home and his fortune becomes the key to success.

Edith Wharton and Kate Chopin described mature women in equally threatened roles. Maturity for a woman means something very different from maturity for a man. All of her early life has been focused on the coming marriage, which has now passed into her memories. Most stories about women stop with the wedding of the ideal couple, noting only that "they lived happily ever after." The new authors, having discovered that there is life after marriage, describe also these middle years for women.

As in the case of the coming-of-age stories, the woman's reality is not considered an appropriate topic for polite literature. The facts are that with marriage and regular sexual activity comes a brand-new phase in life. The staunching of the periodic flow and the mysterious and frightening experience of pregnancy were not nineteenth-century novel topics. For women pregnancy is a time for contemplation and anticipation, a time for preparation for the painful ecstasy of birth. And then comes the joyous pain of birth, and with birth a new separation, again both desired and imposed, and the beginning of a new relationship with a new being that moves from the patterns of bonding to those of individuation. It is symbolized by the cutting of the umbilical cord, an act that must be repeated psychologically and emotionally.

Again, though we know these to be the human activities of these years, they were difficult (in fact, well-nigh impossible) subjects for Victorian authors to discuss. Edith Wharton, a late-nineteenth- and early-twentieth-century American author, who wrote brilliantly of upper-class life in old New York, chose to tell of a courtship and marriage in *The Age of Innocence*. She preferred to narrate much of the story from the hero's point of view. But as we follow his divided love between the good woman he married and the interesting one he prefers, we see the motives for his proper actions and guess at the psychology of these mature women. The wife is a lovely and apparently mindless conformist who seems to be what any sensible man would want. She bears his children, orders his home, entertains his friends, and dies before him. Only after her death does he discover that she has always known of his infidelity and his failure to return her love in full. The cousin (his temptress) who has divorced her husband and elected a childless Bohemian life is always a social outcast. The family, identifying her as a threat, joins forces to drive her away.

Neither life seems happy by modern standards, and neither seems fulfilled. Yet Wharton seems to suggest that these ways were better than the later patterns of self-indulgence. She elects to tell her tale of manners in an ironic, realistic style, as though she were an anthropologist studying an alien culture. Her cool distance brings their passions into relief, capturing gestures and words for our analysis and judgment. Sometimes the effect is of a delicately carved cameo.

Another, more intense, portrayal of the unhappy marriage appears in Kate Chopin's aforementioned *The Awakening.* This book was considered a scandal at the time it was published. It still provokes controversy. The tale focuses on a young wife who is bored with her polite, comfortable life. She abruptly leaves her handsome husband and charming children to try her hand at painting, dabbles in adultery, and finally drowns herself. The tone is languid and confused, mirroring the vague motivations and complex dissatisfactions of the heroine.

If we consider the intense focus on youth in American literature and life, we can understand Wharton's and Chopin's portrayals of restlessness in women entering these middle years. All of the adventure of the Great Husband Hunt is done. Beauty has peaked, and love's magic is diminished. No great conquests seem to loom ahead. Life looks like an endless desert stretching ahead. So why live?

What has the aging woman to contemplate that will lead her to cherish life? The aging mother settled in her empty nest, with her useless womb, is no longer governed by the moon's phases. Her menses have paused, and stopped. Had she lived in an earlier time, this would be the time of her literal death. Among the ancients, the few surviving old women, now barren, became the hags, the witches, the soothsayers, the prophetesses, or the crones.

Certainly old men and old women are rarely the subjects of stories in America. Nonetheless, some modern American authors have selected the aging actors as their protagonists. Ernest Hemingway, the perennial adolescent, revealed his own aging process through a number of novels. The best of these is *The Old Man and the Sea,* a fine novel about an old man and a young boy sharing the delights of nature and the joys of the hunt. In their fierce battle with the great fish, they experience once again the old thrill of the strenuous life that Hemingway so frequently celebrated. Hemingway, always the adventure lover, selects this as the shared dream of youth and age. His man is still the hunter, the human with and against nature. Camaraderie comes from sharing this epic combat.

Eudora Welty, a very different kind of writer, is far more inclined to celebrate the contemplative life, especially in women who are aging. She is also far less individualistic and self-congratulatory than is Ernest Hemingway. She too tells of aging and dying (as well as maturing and bearing) in a novel that is a fascinating contrast to Hemingway's. In *Losing Battles* Welty chooses as her heroine the old schoolteacher in the Mississippi Delta, who like the old fisherman, is also bonded with the youngsters. She too realizes that life is about to stop, for it has been slowing down for years. For this bedridden old woman only her mental life can be strenuous. She too joins forces with the young who are not her natural children, but who catch her spirit and carry forth some of her dreams. This old warrior, confined first to her bed and then to her grave, cannot join the young in search of the great fish. She is the instigator, the facilitator, the chronicler—but not the main actor. Others claim the high offices, make the fortunes, have the grand adventures.

This novel is organized around another old woman's birthday. Granny's big day is a cause for the family celebration. It is also the time of the teacher's death, an occasion for mourning and remembrance. Welty uses the traditional rites of the community, including rituals of eating and initiation and mating and parting. A great lover of folk ways and folk tales, Eudora Welty is attuned to the mythic patterns and activities and uses them throughout her novels and stories, especially in her story of aging. For her, age means wisdom.

Each of these novels uses the forms developed by and for men to tell about the experiences of women. They use different structures because they cover different lives. Yet in each case, we can see clearly the original shape from which they derived. We can also perceive the deeper patterns, the mythic undergirding, in such tales. The very choice of characters that we have been exploring in each of these novels conforms to some classic images. As we study these, we can see still better how much of the wine is new and how genuine the need for new wineskins. (Actually, for the modern reader, we should talk about choosing patterns, cutting clothes to fit a growing body, and ripping out seams to adjust to the changing shapes. Seamstress images are more immediate for most of us than vineyard images.)

Classic and Contemporary Modes

Folk literature often portrays the stages of the woman's life — the maiden, the wife, and the crone, the three faces of Eve. The three goddesses who tempt Paris are lust (Aphrodite), power (Hera), and wisdom (Athena). It is no surprise that the young man would have selected the pubescent female image, in conformity with his own natural stage of development. How many young men have the foresight to choose power or the maturity to choose wisdom? Literature, whether written by men or by women, usually reflects the combination of natural patterns, cultural givens, and prevailing world-views.

In Hebrew literature the blood whose ebb and flow marks the phases of female life is seen as filth. According to Mosaic Law, the woman who is menstruating or has just given birth is "unclean." Until she has undergone a ritual cleansing, she is forbidden to the God-fearing man. The prohibition is probably a protection for the woman, but the imagery that equates blood with filth has lingered to haunt the modern. Certainly it would explain the long absence of discussions of women's great physical changes. It also explains, in part, the slow development of literature among female Jewish writers. The low status of the female, her uncleanness, her role as handmaiden to the male, all make her an unlikely author or subject of literature.

The law of Moses has lost much of its authority among the moderns. Christ altered the status of women and washed away forever the image of female filth. He did not hesitate to heal the woman suffering from the bloody flux (Mark 5:25–34). His followers have accepted the Incarnation as the basis for revising their view of the whole process of birth. If Christ was born of woman, then neither birth nor woman could ever again be unclean. They also have a new respect for the flesh—now clearly united with the spirit—as it became the garment for God Himself. And finally, Christians have a new respect for the arts, now harnessed for use by the faithful.

The ancient power of the Mother Goddess, while lingering into modern times, has also seen a historical transformation. Even though the post-Renaissance world has seen the rise of science and the decline of mysticism, woman has retained some of her ties with witchcraft and nature. The ancient identification with nature—with the fertile land and the teeming sea, which also ebbs and flows in obedience to the phases of the moon—remains, along with the imagery of mystery and darkness. But she no longer need be seen as the passive life force, the world's womb. Since the new science has prolonged life beyond menopause and found means for interrupting the rhythms of fertility, woman is no longer necessarily burdened (or blessed) by tribes of children and doomed to fade with her fertility. She may be judged less as a receptive part of nature and more as an actor and an individual, capable of living her own life, making her own choices, and telling her own story.

As a result, some recent stories break with polite tradition to present new images of female experience. They demonstrate contrasting artistic choices from those in the more classic tales that we have been considering. In *The Bell Jar* the exciting, thoughtful, but directionless young author Sylvia Plath tells a distinctly autobiographical story of a young woman who feels she must leave home and have her first sexual encounter before she begins to understand who she is. This is more like the traditional hero than the traditional heroine. If this had been a nineteenth-century novel, the ending would have been her "fall"—a justification for ostracism or death. But for the so-called independent and unconventional twentieth-century American girl, the fall becomes a new beginning—a new awareness. Yet even here the adventures are not as impressive as the man's. Her climax is more likely to be sexual, suggesting that even women without Christian values of chastity continue to identify the loss of virginity as a significant threshold—the moment of initiation. She has won a great opportunity to go to New York, to work for a fashion magazine, to have a new wardrobe. Plath's heroine discovers that none of this is very wonderful. She tells her story as a recollection. Now her baby is playing with the baubles that were once stylish fashions. She demonstrates her values as she cuts the ornaments off a pair of old sunglasses and hands them to her children to enjoy. The very fact that the novel moves beyond romance to maturity gives it a new focus and a fresh meaning.

While the older novels ended with the heroine happily married to the proper hero at the appropriate level of fortune, the modern woman's novel may start with marriage or it may not include marriage at all. The bed, which was the woman's making or breaking in earlier tales, may be nothing more than another piece of furniture in a modern crowded life. The sexual encounter can be as casual as an early supper with a stranger. If it ends in marriage, that is by no means the conclusion of life. Women continue to live their lives after marriage and to have needs that are more complex than the need to bear children. Their adventures are becoming more diverse, reflecting the changing times. The focus is therefore less obsessively on their sexual purity and more on the full range of their human experiences.

Take, for example, a recent novel by Shirley Hazzard, *The Transit of Venus*.[82] Here we see two Australian sisters who choose quite different paths in life. Neither becomes a great success on her own. One marries young and is faithful to a stuffy English civil servant who dominates her without ever sensing her needs. At one point she falls desperately in love with a young Scot doctor who is caring for her son. They glow and stutter and dream of one another while behaving with great self-control and delicacy. Then he forces himself to leave, and she goes back to her role of good wife and mother. Neither her husband nor her children ever have a clue of the romance that has stirred her heart. They see only the plump and innocent household furnishing. We see a woman who continues to struggle with her own needs long after the family and the outside world have classified her and filed her away.

Her more adventuresome sister Cara rejects a scientist who loves her with passion and incredible endurance. She turns instead to a cynical, sophisticated, and immoral young poet, giving him her love and her body without any hope that he will treat her as more than a back-alley lover. When he marries an aristocratic woman and finds that she is pregnant, he abandons Cara. She suffers terribly from his rejection of her love, but she survives to love again. She herself remains childless throughout the novel. Years later, after Cara has found another kind of love with another kind of man, one who is solid and decent and thoughtful and noble, she comes to see her poet for the shallow, brittle person that he really is—all artificiality and decadence.

He has used both her and his wife in a perverse game to hide his own homosexual affairs. His life becomes like a circle in Dante's hell, with his own choices turning back on themselves, returning in his only son to haunt him. At last after her husband's death Cara returns to her first lover (the scientist) but seeks to protect his wife. For Cara love has strong moral concerns, though her early life seems that of the loose woman. The book is a beautiful study of the forms that love takes, the stages of women's lives, and the consequent systems of values that one embraces. Incidents that might seem insignificant return to haunt the imagination. It is a delicate description of two women climbing love's ladder, only to find that the ladder is really a path that endlessly circles back on itself.

Without preaching, Shirley Hazzard presents moral choices and examines ethical values. She allows evil to work itself out, building its own damnation. The seekers after good, in spite of nettles along the way, have the rewards of good conscience and continuing relationships. None of the characters is completely pure, and none is a simple type. This is a rich example of a talented woman using her understanding and her craft to build an excellent novel.

Following through a book like this, which chronicles decades in women's lives, we sense a pattern—the different stages of life. Shakespeare spoke of the ages of man. A novelist like Hazzard is discovering parallel stages for woman, starting with the coming of age, moving through the adolescent search and experiment into the settled period of marriage or single maturity, and ending in peace and death. The very epic scope contrasts with the classic focus on youth, as if female life were truncated.

Edith Wharton's *The House of Mirth* also captures the epic quality of female life. The novel starts with a lively young woman, Lily Bart, who is talented and charming. At the height of her beauty she finds that the appropriate "catch" is boring and pretentious. Marriage to him would be a form of entombment. With hardly a second thought she turns her attentions to a livelier man who offers no real potential for marriage and no real support. Another more practical proposition by an older man seems to her unthinkable. She continues her thoughtless and proud decisions until she finds herself without resources. By then her suitors have disappeared or changed their minds. As

Lily whirls about the giddy world of New York and European social life, she erroneously concludes that her looks and her personal charm are enough to make her fortune and to keep her safe forever. Practical plotting and compromise and self-control seem too dreary for such as she.

Gradually doors close to her and opportunities slip away. She finds herself without income or hope, and she realizes too late that the woman without property must be shrewd and ruthless to survive. Poor Lily! She has no talent for deception or survival. She is too fastidious to consider relationships that other women accept as a practical solution. Nor has she the income to maintain a place in the fashionable world that she earlier sneered at. She has neither family nor friends on whom she may rely. She has no marketable skills. After her glitter and elegance have dimmed, she struggles to earn a living in a hat shop. Soon she finds that common laborers are far superior to her; she has not even the most primitive marketable skills. Unable to adapt or to learn or to accept the rules of a hostile world, she finally fades away—alone and desolate.

The book is a brilliant study of an aging belle who lacks the tough practicality essential for coping with life. An idealist too blind to spot even her own flaws, she criticizes others and laughs herself out of polite society. For a woman so much a creature of society, this blindness proves fatal. The novel is written in the tragic mode; following the classic falling action, her inevitable doom results from character rather than chance. The violence all turns against society and self. It is the ideal shape for the woman's tragedy—based on a hubris that grows from beauty and charm, ending in ostracism and self-destruction. Wharton's cool, controlled style is a powerful form to enclose such a tale.

Another example of a typical modern heroine of women's novels is the leading character in Virginia Woolf's *Mrs. Dalloway*. The story is told from Mrs. Dalloway's point of view as she lives through a single day. It has as its climax a dinner party that she is planning for the evening. Not a classic heroine, Mrs. Dalloway is middle-aged, moderately attractive, fairly wealthy, and not especially interested in adulterous intrigues. She has married a man she loves and has no vast ambitions for a life beyond the one she is living. She is not on the verge of any particular rite of passage. Like most of us, she is just living out one day that is not very different from any other day. Nor does much happen—as is the case with most of our days. She goes about town planning her menu, buying the flowers for the table, dressing for the event, chatting with the guests. And as she does these things, she touches—without noticing it—a world full of much greater forces. A war victim who also lives in London shares her space and time without attracting her attention. At one point in the story their lives cross and at another his story breaks in on her consciousness. But he is at best tangential to her life. Heads of state may mingle with her guests, but she does not discuss international matters with them. This is a charming woman who knows neither secrets of state nor horrors of war. She knows only about servants and china and floral arrangements and matters of the heart. Nothing heroic or romantic lends glamour to this modest tale of modest scale.

Students reading this novel invariably express their outrage at the triviality of its concerns—even though they would have to acknowledge that their own lives are full of equally trivial concerns. Even when these students study the aesthetic basis for these choices, the way that we perceive life as a shower of tiny sensory experiences, they are unhappy that Woolf did not construct a neat linear narrative about really "important" issues. Though they may see their own lives as a host of petty concerns, they are cross with her for refusal to face the "big" issues of life and death. Yet the seating arrangement for a dinner party may well be the big issue that a woman faces in her day. If young scholars or angry feminists insist that this is silly stuff, that her party is worthless, then they are denigrating her life and value. After all, at the same time, the culture is insisting that this is woman's proper work, that she stay home and prepare such parties. We may in fact be suggesting that both her life and her work need to be either revalued or altered. Perhaps no one should be spending her entire life on activities rated as petty by the rest of the world, but certainly each life contains many such details.

Obviously reading such a novel does call into question our definition of worth. Is the activity of men, by definition, important because it is done by men? Is the work of women also by definition inconsequential because it is performed by women? The work routinely thrust on women tends to be repetitive, dull, and nonliterary. Childbearing, diaper changing, food preparing, not to mention cleaning, washing, scrubbing, dusting, shopping, chauffeuring—these are all essential to those who must be born and eat and work and learn. But most of these activities are also constant reminders of our base and fallen nature. No wonder the hero scorns those very functions that obsess the average woman. What hero is pictured with wet diapers or dirty dishes? The hero, by his elevated spiritual nature, does not need access to either the bathroom or the kitchen. Home, in fact, is the place that he leaves in order to be heroic.

In novels like those by Virginia Woolf, we often see the baser concerns sublimated—perhaps because of her own class and life style. Childless, she had little concern for diapers or nursing problems. Wealthy, she had little occasion to scrub a floor or a pan. In a more elegant, antiseptic way, she selects a flower or a dish. The servants allow her to be quietly feminine without being grossly female. This ideal of womanliness serves as the core of Woolf's novels. She tends to avoid any criticism of the wasted days of such ladies, but in *To the Lighthouse,* she does juxtapose this life with the more vigorous path of the artist. In neither case does she suggest that the life has any value beyond the tissue of experiences and relationships and feelings for this moment in time. Her world, for all of its subtle elegance, is limited to physical existence on earth and to individual choices. Inevitably, she would focus on beauty and love.

Much of woman's attention is given to making herself attractive and her home inviting. The physical beauty that is widely celebrated in lyric poetry is as brief as the rose. From the moment it starts to fade, she is inclined to preen and paint and dress and decorate herself in order to maintain the vanishing image of youth and beauty. Our culture tends to view the mature man as impressive, but the mature woman as repellent. The qualities for which a woman has traditionally been cherished, her physical beauty and her childbearing capacity, are at war with each other. In her courtship she is the subject of romantic sonnets and the object of adoration. In her lusty maturity she may be the partner in erotic narratives. But childbearing and breast-feeding soon wear away the lithe curves that thrilled the eye. And her very accessibility and vulnerability breed contempt. The burden of housework drags the perennial mother into premature middle age and early death.

Most novels, like Woolf's, deal with the middle or upper classes, not with the lower. Such women can delay their trip down this inevitable path of physical deterioration, though their efforts become increasingly grotesque. Even here, age threatens the heroine far more than it does the hero.

Furthermore, the woman who allows herself to become isolated from the mainstream of life—a sequestering that many cultures have encouraged—may become a perennial adolescent. She may be slow to develop the compensatory maturity of mind and breadth of experience that make the mature hero celebrated for his increasing wisdom. The older heroine becomes a bore largely because she has been denied access to the rich discussion of "significant" ideas that men of the world routinely share. Even in our more egalitarian culture, men and women often separate after dinner. The tacit assumption seems to be that men would prefer talk about politics and work and sports, while women enjoy discussions of children and household appliances. (One might wonder what makes sports more significant than children.) Women plan parties and plot weddings, but men decide on the wars. Consider the conversations in Jane Austen's households. No wonder women seem so silly. They have rarely had easy conversance with those parts of life that the dominant sex has chosen to value.

In fact (as mentioned earlier), Jane Austen, with all of her wit and ability, is reported to have laughed at the very suggestion that she might write an epic. She insisted that her talents lay in chronicling the activity on the two square inches of ivory she knew so thoroughly. The Napoleonic Wars, which occupied the men of her day, could not fit into her two inches. Without experience of life's grand adventures, women cannot describe them with any authority.

Of course, all literature is not epic in scope. Good novels have been written about men doing quite unheroic things—farming and sailing and fishing. And, of late, good novels have been written by Edith Wharton or Willa Cather or Eudora Welty about the daily activities of men and women—eating their meals and raising their children and facing the elements as best they can. For the great mass of both men and women, more of life is like Willa Cather's frontier stories than Hemingway's bullfights. Men may share a few exciting and horrible war experiences, but most have never had a fist fight with a killer or hunted wild animals in Africa. Most men, like most women, know tiny victories at school and at work and at home. Most of us consider that a promotion or a new child is enough to content us for quite a while. We do not need the search for the Golden Fleece if our children are healthy and we have found satisfying work.

Nor do most of us marry the gorgeous man or woman who inhabits heroic fiction and film. We marry the decent person next door—warts and all—who is a comfortable companion through life, who shares our joy and our sorrow, and who does not expect us to measure up to filmic heroism or beauty.

Furthermore, most of us do not really see life as a series of dramatic events. We focus on one point after another, hardly seeing how they are related. Those events that matter to women indeed may be very different from the public ones that matter more to men. Eudora Welty is especially effective in showing how a woman in a traditional culture can demonstrate her love of the family through cooking. To celebrate the return of a child, she might bake a cake. To show displeasure with the husband, she might leave cold leftovers. Rather than speech, she may use the weapons of silence or absence. Women commonly use the weapons of the traditionally weak portion of society: they may seek to convince through indirection, making emotions the instrument of their will. (Even Esther asked the key question of her king after she dressed elegantly and fed him well.) Powerless people dare not risk frontal assault; they instead often use devious lateral actions. And they may use every weapon at hand—beauty, wit, and a thorough understanding of male psychology. The serf has strong motives for studying the mind-set of the overlord. It is the better part of valor and for his own benefit for the serf to use the lord's preferences against himself. Such an oblique angle of vision produces a very different story from the forthright telling that is more common in masculine literature.

Plotting Life and Values

If we look back over our lives, most of us have trouble seeing a single line of progression building to a neat climax with a recognition scene and a reversal. In fact, each moment is so full of a number of things and the moments follow one another in such a rush that we are puzzled to discover any patterns to life. Sometimes life seems more like a web than a neat line with clear motivation and cause-and-effect relationships.

Not only the plot line of "life," but the level of activity may also need reevaluation. Given this mundane existence we live, full of small contentments and fuzzy motivation, why do we choose to honor war and brutality? A study of history is rarely more than a narrative of violent men seeking power and property for selfish motives. Years of peace and prosperity seldom capture our attention like the flash of the assassin's bullet. The billions of women who have borne, raised, and married the billions of men that have made this history are seldom more than a footnote in most books. They were often the partners or the victims of this cavalcade of history, but history reduces their numbers to that handful who acted like men. Cleopatra or Elizabeth or Victoria can get into the books and enter the imagination as images of power. Their sisters and aunts and nieces and daughters, however, are as nameless as the other daughters of Eve—unless they too assume powerful roles. The answer is simple: we do not bestow honor on powerless, peaceful people who do their work and love their husbands and raise law-abiding children. We prefer to discuss those who lure one another's husbands into adultery or who wrest power away from others or who turn their children into power brokers.

The issue is interesting for women's studies. The search for an authentic female voice may turn out to be the beginning of a revolution in values. Gentle people who love the land and who have talents for nurturing may become the new central figures of our stories. Virginia Woolf pointed the way in *To the Lighthouse*. Her heroine achieves very little, but she does draw together a circle of love. The characters never undertake the mini-epic voyage of the title, which would have been a modest endeavor at best. The novel is almost static. The main event is skipped, and the death of the heroine is passed over and recounted from memory. Woolf is forcing her readers into a more meditative and less active form.

Realistically this is the actual life style for most of us. We tend to circle about life, trying to understand how and why we live. We are frequently thrust into activities that have no clear beginning and end. We rarely understand the significance of the things we do until long after they are done. And our moments of greatest heroism may seem almost comic in retrospect. The absurdity and confusion of much of human life are not properly described in the simplistic form of the neat plot. And for women the potential for heroic stature or action has been so minimal that the image of the Winged Victory seems wildly overstated. As Willa Cather shows us in her portrayals of strong women who lived frontier lives on the plains of the American Midwest, female heroism is usually stoic and unchronicled.

Vividly illustrating this quality of quiet feminine strength and fortitude is an excellent frontier story by novelist and short-story writer Caroline Gordon (1895–1981). In "The Captive" a young wife left alone in a cabin in Kentucky finds herself facing a band of hostile Indians. They loot and burn her belongings and finally take her and her baby captive. The Indians drag them on a forced march over many miles. She watches as they bash out her baby's brains and accepts silently the experience of the tribe's males bartering for her. She learns to live as an Indian and to avoid the more painful violations. In time she is liberated, but we know that only her toughness kept her alive and sane.

The clear, unemotional tone of the story contrasts with the violent actions. Reading in it, we share experiences with the women who pioneered this country, working hand in hand with their frontier husbands. Such fiction allows us to step outside our skins and live another life in another era.

Among the most effective chroniclers of the modest life of the average citizen are the modern writers of the American South. Mississippian William Faulkner (1897–1962), winner of the Nobel Prize for literature in 1949, wrote of the old, universal truths, the eternal verities, and the struggles and conflicts within the human heart. He saw the greatness in little things and the littleness in great things. He found tragedy in the death and burial of a poor white woman. He found comedy in the death of a swashbuckling Civil War officer. A black woman who watched a white family go through its theatrical gestures proved to be more powerful and heroic than any of the elegant ladies or grand gentlemen. The beauty of the human spirit is not limited to those who look heroic but extends to those who have inner strength.

Two modern southerners who carry this tradition even further

are Flannery O'Connor and Eudora Welty. In the life and letters
of Flannery O'Connor, we have a vision of a valiant spirit that
refuses to flatter itself with big names for commonplace actions.
Her suffering from a degenerative condition over the years, her
passionate love of nature, her comic vision of the people around
her, her vivid imagination, and her heroic fidelity to her faith
made her a remarkable literary figure. *The Habit of Being* is a
moving experience for the reader who knows the life behind
these gallant letters, the pain behind these comic lines. Believing
that she and the people around her are not beautiful heroes and
heroines, but fallen men and women, O'Connor takes a tough
look at human deformity. The fat woman whom the world would
call "poor white trash" may be a child of God blessed with
visionary power. The wealthy and the proud landowner who
sneers at her may have her feet placed firmly on the path to
damnation. The polite Bible salesman can be as depraved as the
one-legged doctor of philosophy. The human spirit is deeper than
appearance or education or class can explain. Behind these
twisted figures with their ritualistic speech is the old battle of the
angels. A woman, for example, can point proudly to a field and
claim it for her own. Or she can call a hired man her "savior."
And in these words, we know that she is tragically wrong. She
must recognize her error or face damnation. Simple actions take
on a symbolic significance to O'Connor because they point to the
corruption of the heart or the purity of the spirit.

The Christian reader will find in this tough-minded and wise
writer both insights and idiosyncratic approaches that are
disturbing and thrilling. She looks beyond questions of stereotype and male-female roles to the basic questions of human
destiny—the same questions that had been addressed by Dante
and Milton.

A more gentle writer is Eudora Welty. She too is concerned
with the timeless, universal issues of human life, but her
chronicles are less grotesque than O'Connor's. She finds her
stories in the common stuff of life. She loves to write about the
materials of the woman's life: weddings and births and deaths,
dresses and arguments and recipes. As noted earlier, she sees the
grandeur of the insignificant life in *Losing Battles*. The old-maid
schoolteacher who has just died was, in the eyes of the world, a
failure. She never found herself a rich husband—or any

husband. She never made much money or moved to a better school. She never dressed very well. Her best students either dropped out or left to become successes elsewhere. When it comes time for her to die, her nurse will not even let her die the way she wants. She takes away the teacher's pencil and paper so that the dying woman cannot write to those she wants to send final messages. Yet the accumulated losses of her life tally up to a massive victory. Out of the hard red clay soil of Mississippi has come a loving and sensitive and intelligent and indomitable spirit who has never bowed before the forces that surround her. She continues to fight ignorance and sloth, not even considering that she can never win. Taking a character that would have been a caricature in anyone else's hands, Eudora Welty follows the sexless spinster's life to a beautiful fulfillment. Finally an old woman, who is not a mother, is portrayed as beautiful and heroic.

Eudora Welty's stories are often portraits of those characters whom other authors would have ignored. She takes freaks and spinsters and makes them seem important. What fascinates her is the truth that lies below the surface. Certainly Christian readers can sympathize with this love of life's alienated peoples.

Simone de Beauvoir has noted that one of the most compelling truths of women is their sense of being the "other." Normal life is male life. All others are "non-male." Thus whatever makes a woman different from a man also makes her inferior to him. Only by being adjunct to man (as wife or mother) can the woman appear normal. Thus the woman alone is a freak. This in turn can build bonds of sympathy with life's misfits, allowing great opportunities for companionship and understanding.

For a number of modern women authors, the shape of the novel is that of surfaces and depths—an image of water. The artist is one who dives deep and surfaces, bringing up from the depths of experience strange and beautiful truths. The male pattern of the swimmer is the Byronic athlete who swims the Hellespont—that is, he has a goal in mind, an achievement.[83] But the woman may use the symbol as a baptismal pattern for rebirth and wisdom. The old ties with nature take on new dimensions.

In any event, we have learned that analyzing the plot of a story involves more than simply studying a series of events and their interrelationships. Selecting the events, ordering them, revealing them in a specific way, and giving them value—all of these have meaning.

The sensitive reader must watch to see what the author is asking him or her to explore and to applaud. Literature is a reflection of life and a lamp by which we see life and a map by which we chart it. We must not accept blindly the values of every artist whom we read. Especially when the author seems to denigrate our lives and our values and the people whom we respect and value, we should look closely at the rejection or the denigration and consider the underlying philosophic rationale.

If women's literature can make us all reconsider why warriors are heroic and nurturers are not, why adultery is thrilling and fidelity is not, why youth is admirable and age is not, then women writers have done great good. Literature that reflects the pagan, materialistic, violent, and superficial values of the society is far more prevalent than that which mirrors the spiritual concerns of wise people. It has reinforced an empty-headed activism, a quick and superficial judgment of human value. It is well to step back and compare a violent, sensual story with our own lives and our own values and then decide—no matter how impressive the craft or style—whether we applaud the ideas. And these ideas are themselves often hidden in the character and the form of the story. Reading of such a sort cannot be the easy assimilation of impressions that most of us prefer. It is tough work for an active and creative reader.

chapter seven

So, What's New?
And What's Good?

The author shows the differences between art and craft, discussing the task of the reader as critic and providing suggestions for judging modern literature by and about women.

Everything, it would seem, has been made new. Women's literature has erupted in the world as a natural force of breathtaking power. And it is affecting that world in dramatic—as well as subtle—ways. The very nature of language is changing, not only in literature but in daily discourse. *He/she, human*kind rather than *man*kind, *persons* rather than *men*—these are daily experiences as we seek to assimilate the ideas of the movement into a new vocabulary and attitude. These words, in turn, are used by both men and women to describe a host of new characters, new to literature though hardly new to our experience. And these characters act out lives that break the stereotypes of traditional literature, thereby offering insights and thematic changes that are fresh and exciting, though not always acceptable.

Our task as active readers who care about the works that we read is to understand the changes, to decide the level of their

117

aesthetic power, and to judge their relevance and their accuracy and their value for us. Christian liberty demands this of us.

The New Story for Women

The traditional story in Western literature has focused on the young girl, a passive creature as a rule, who is lovely and vulnerable and imperiled. The story is most often focused on the goal of marriage—that dangerous transfer from one set of protectors to another. It may deal with the efforts of the parents to thwart a romance or to encourage one. A collision of wills may result in estrangement and isolation; the young innocent may make the wrong choices of paths or persons. The threat is usually sexual; the danger involves becoming a "fallen woman." It is a very limited feminine version of Edenic innocence and the first faltering steps toward the snake and the world east of Eden.

Even with this new literature appearing by and about women, no one denies that marriage is still the central event in most women's lives. No other choice comes close in determining a woman's earthly fate.

But now we see more stories about alternative paths: single women, divorced women, disillusioned wives walking away from boring marriages. Instead of being passive victims or blessed recipients, women seem more in charge of their destinies, more active in making conscious choices. In some ways, this takes a bit of the drama out of the romances, because women are no longer "stuck" with marriage no matter what the circumstances.

More and more of the stories now focus on life after marriage: fading romance, the birth of the first child, the problems of the empty nest. With the change in the work picture, women have found paths outside of marriage and the home. Married women now deal with their dissatisfaction by choosing new careers or returning to old ones. They may choose to place marriage or a love affair in a secondary position. With the massive sociological changes and the radical moral transformations in modern life, such stories are bound to proliferate.

By shifting from the straight line action leading to the marriage or gutter to the more meandering pattern of second thoughts and confused motives, authors have changed the whole tone of the woman's novel. Martha Quest of Doris Lessing's novels is a seeker without clear notions of her goal.[84] Like the characters in Virginia Woolf's novels, she is more likely to drift from one meaningless event to another, seeking in vain to wrest some meaning out of them. This all suggests that life is a process of stumbling into decisions and tumbling into and out of relationships. Such a world-view contains less conscious decision making than stream-of-consciousness and fog. Women in many of the more interesting contemporary novels face a steady stream of dreary alternatives, as formless as modern life and leading nowhere.

Although this view is a common one among older adults, particularly women who believe their choices make no significant difference, it is hardly a view that can be embraced by Christian readers. If we are to lead lives with meaning, we need to have a reason for existence, a center to that existence. We need to know that we are God's creatures, made in His image, redeemed, capable of communion with Him, worthy of His love, living lives that He can use for His purposes. We do need meaningful work to fill those lives, and most of us need other people in fairly stable relationships. We also need change, growth, a sense of fulfillment. God has promised us: that we are here to glorify Him and to serve Him, that we can mature in the faith, that we can win battles for Him, that our quest can have meaning. When we seek, we shall find.

If we are to believe a host of modern novelists, we should expect no pattern or meaning to our lives in the secular city. If such novels are truly a mirror of modern life, then the sense of God's strong hand guiding human lives is now rare. The health and sanity of *The Confessions of St. Augustine* have given way to a sterile celebration of self, where no God leads and only self-gratification seems significant. And that, in turn, leads only to a meaningless meander through the absurd labyrinth that we call life. The current elevation of existential writing is part of this trend away from absolutes and road maps and dependable divine guidance.

The classic tales often focused on the first awakening of the young girl with her first experience of love and life. Certainly this theme still dominates romantic fiction, but alternatives are increasingly apparent. Marriage is not always an option for women. Sayers noted, for example, that the choice was not a real one for many English women after the First World War, in which a large percentage of the men were killed. The women were forced to find a way to live by themselves and then to find meaning in those lives. With the nuclear family of the modern era, the alternatives for the unwed woman are quite different from those available in earlier history. Woman increasingly needs to learn to deal with the life beyond the cloister. For her the path is not simply to the altar, but through pain to salvation or damnation. The sin of the youth may or may not lead to marriage. It may instead prove the basis for the "fortunate fall,"[85] resulting in her greater depth of understanding and maturity.

More and more modern fiction is touching on the second awakening for woman. This second experience comes to the mature person, now lined and aging. She is growing weary of her busy husband and her demanding children, feeling useless in a home that is increasingly empty much of the day. She can find little gratification in scrubbing her immaculate floors or in redecorating her already elegant parlor. The round of beauty shops and grocery stores, bridge luncheons and PTA meetings, has grown stale. Her temptation is to seek adventure—usually through adultery with a neighbor or a friend or a stranger she meets at random. This plot pattern titillates readers, but does not ring true or satisfying to many women.

Kate Chopin, for example, suggests that adultery is not a long-lasting answer for the seeking woman. The heroine of Chopin's book *The Awakening* loses her reputation without gaining any new sense of direction. Others who have no interest in the moral implications wonder why adultery is even a concern. With the prevailing attitude toward sexuality, most fiction treats sexual adventure as exciting but neither permanent nor significant. Again, the Christian with traditional views about the body as the temple of the Holy Spirit may have deep doubts about such implicit or explicit ideas in modern literature.

Certainly the mid-life crisis can be a very real experience for both men and women and is a popular issue in modern literature. Women who had chosen marriage frequently turn to college and career, looking for the path missed earlier. Some such late starters are delighted at the very experiences that would have bored them at an earlier age. But this new beginning may have a wrenching effect on the other relationships that are in place, and the expectations of the family and the world. It may upset the children and ruin the marriage. But many families are finding ways to cope with the new relationships and the new sense of worth. It behooves the Christian to judge carefully such stories of the exciting new life in a career. (Many are filled with unreal glamour. Women tend to rise from rags to riches within minutes in these new Horatio Alger stories.) We must be careful to balance our private needs against those of the family and the obligations that we owe to our Lord. We are not our own persons. For us, men and women alike, self-fulfillment often lies in sacrifice and in service. The female who flirts her way to the top, proud of her new wardrobe and power, is hardly a model for the Christian life. Mammon, who can come dressed as either man or woman, needs to be clearly identified.

While the old goal of women recounted in the tales was for the ideal man, the more common goal in the modern tale is for self-fulfillment. Women are increasingly asking themselves, "Who am I?"

For the Christian man or woman the answer is clear: we are children of God, considered worth the sacrifice of His only begotten Son. We are precious to Him whether or not we have lives of glitter and power. Worth comes from this primary relationship, not from such trivial pursuits as career and education and home improvement. All of these must be viewed in the context of our higher calling to be children of God, instruments of His purpose. We can serve in the kitchen or the craftshop or the board room. So long as we allow the world to establish our values, we are doomed to meaningless lives. Trends become everything. We need to look in others' eyes to see mirrors of ourselves and determine how we look. The real liberation for Christian women is in being free to be what God wants them to be. He has promised that then we shall have life and have it in abundance. For this we do not need shiny linoleum, Dior clothing, or lunches with executives.

Although we insist that the modern novel has moved somewhat away from the beautiful young maiden lost in the forest, we must admit that America is still youth oriented. The aging heroine remains a rarity. (And "aging" often means merely over thirty.) The middle-aged heroine with a career of her own is still an oddity in novels, though she occasionally appears in films. Perhaps the abundance of talented aging actresses has encouraged stories like *All About Eve* or *Sunset Boulevard* or *Sweet Bird of Youth*. An especially beautiful film about middle-aged women and their choices was *The Turning Point*.[86] This film showed two women, one of whom chose marriage and family, and the other a career in dance. Each faces the crises of age: the mother will lose her children, the dancer will lose her place in the spotlight. Each is now at the turning point, the mid-life crisis, that will take her into the mature years. The decisions each makes will determine whether those remaining years will be rich with meaning and dignity or bitter with anger and resentment.

Earlier novelists tended to prefer writing about the fragile woman, as well as the youthful one. But contemporary writers, even many male writers, are increasingly interested in tougher, more authoritative females. Especially in stories by black authors do we find the powerful woman; the writer Maya Angelou is herself such a figure, and Alice Walker tells of strong black female characters. Caroline Gordon told of the frontier woman, capable of fighting beside her husband to protect their children and surviving alone in an alien culture.

Now with the New Woman coming into prominence, this assertive figure may be the career woman fighting for power in a man's world. Power is always interesting in fiction. Whether in men or women, it attracts our attention. Again, the Christian's concern must be the basis of that power and the use of it. Is the assertiveness all for self? Is it a form of pride? Or does it serve a deeper purpose, calling attention to larger concerns, forcing the opposition to new perceptions? The modern world no longer considers the strong woman crazy, but we need not leap too quickly into naming her blessed. We need to recall that the first shall be last, suggesting that all of us, men and women alike, should be fighting for the last place in line on this earth, seeking with all our hearts to encourage others to take the first place and to fulfill themselves. Self-centered philosophies are not appropriate in Christendom.

Woman's Story as Seen by Men

One of the pleasanter effects of the heightened sensitivity to women's concerns is the wave of new writing by men that reflects this sensitivity. While the reputation of macho writers, such as Ernest Hemingway or Norman Mailer,[87] may have declined in some circles, the reputations of other, more androgynous, talents have arisen. While there have been men who are sensitive to the needs of both men and women since the days of Homer, they tend to have somewhat more encouragement today. Such men can obviously have sensitivity without forgetting their sexual identity. They are discovering in themselves the virtues traditionally thought to characterize women—sensitivity, imagination, nurturing, and nonverbal communication skills. Increasingly the writers of both sexes are discovering that the world is not as rational or compartmentalized as it has often been portrayed in much of literature.

In much of modern literature, for example, comedy mingles chaotically with tragedy. Some authors have noted that soldiers in modern stories are displaying less and less interest in being heroes. Their reasons for fighting are not necessarily rational, and their declarations of a separate peace are not necessarily cowardly. The good people of the world do not necessarily emerge victorious. Nor can victory always be achieved by force; rather it may be obtained through a series of small skirmishes that end in a dubious peace. The heroism of the past can seem as absurd to contemporary readers. Yet women generally have not accepted heroism as the flashy masculine ideal, and they have grown accustomed to the idea that the issues they consider important may be perceived as trivial by the history writers or fiction writers. For centuries they have lived in a kind of absurd world of their own, the landscape of a nightmare, a cloud cuckoo land, but they have found ways to make sense of it and to discover their own quiet moments of heroism.

Long ago Christ showed humankind that He did not come as the conquering warrior. God Himself entered the world as a child, a victim of important men like Herod and Caesar. He chose to ride on the foal of an ass rather than the white stallion of the conquering hero. Because He was a man of peace, He was led to the cross to be crucified between two thieves. He took the little actions of life (the washing of feet, the pouring of wine, the breaking of bread) and turned them into the triumphant symbols of victory over the archenemy, Death. Christ, the most liberated of all men, knew the woman's story because He knew the entire human story. As the great artist who turned ideas into flesh, He showed us by His actions and through His parables that human values were all askew. If we look carefully, much of our guidance in judging literature can come from a contemplation of Christ.

The modern sensitive male writer can make the woman a hero as John Irving does in *The World According to Garp*.[88] He can make the man a househusband, the wife the professional achiever, the athlete a transvestite, and the children the wise and rational members of the household. He can celebrate the gentle virtues and break up stereotyped sex roles. And we can appreciate him for the reversals of his novels as well as their comedy. But we need to mitigate our appreciation with an awareness that he lacks transcendent vision. Death is the end for his people. Human love and sensitivity are the highest goods. The family is the only community. This is a humanistic vision of enormous power, but it falls far short of the redeeming power of Christ. We can enjoy such a writer for the humanity he expresses and the sensitivity that he reveals without swallowing his world-view. Obviously such a caveat is important in reading both male and female writers; we should be sensitive critics, sorting out carefully those elements that we find new and good.

The Reader as Critic

After God finished with His creation, each of the days of creation, He assessed His work and decided that it was good. Even after the birth of Christ and His early life, God the Father judged His work, noting that this was His Son in whom He was well pleased. The critical intelligence is at the core of our faith. When Jesus admonished us not to judge, He spoke only of other people's sins, not of life or of art. In fact, He was very clear in condemning the error of the Pharisees' ideas and the money-changers' activities. Christianity is a faith that includes many ideas and forms, but it also excludes many ideas and forms. In literature as in life, the Christian must make subtle judgments about the intellectual food he or she will relish.

For example, in the novels of Irving or the poetry of Adrienne Rich, we can appreciate the sensitivity, expressiveness, and freshness; we can respond to the ideas and the craftsmanship;

but we can also reject the world-view and the behavior.[89] In order to do this, we need to become aware of the levels on which a work may be judged and of the appropriate tools for judgment.

Art and Craft

Numerous times in this book the term *craft* has appeared, often in a derogatory manner. The ancient Greeks saw craftsmen as artisans of the lower classes. The true artist was likely to be the worker in words and ideas, not the worker in stone or clay. In another context the creation of the hands of women, pottery or needlework or weaving, was perceived as decorative or utilitarian, lacking the lofty significance of true art. It would seem that craft is the commonplace use of material for construction, while art is the more imaginative and spiritual use of physical properties to appeal more powerfully and aesthetically. Actually, the difference is quite arbitrary. If we consider a work mechanical or unimaginative, we are most likely to call it "merely craft." We may decide that art cannot be useful or derivative or simple or whatever. These are subjective determinations, based on our own cultural biases and on certain private prejudices. The work we really like we often decide is "real art."

Aside from such semantic differences, craft—good workmanship—is basic to good art. The artist usually starts by learning the tools of her trade and ends by bringing imagination and inspiration to the work so that it transcends time and place, communicating with power to people that the artist never will meet in person. In literature the artist forces the imaginative reader to participate in her experience.

Much that is written is not well constructed; it is clumsy and crude craftsmanship. In addition it may lack any spark of creative power. It is like the inert flesh of Adam before God breathed life into him. Talent can be obvious in a work that lacks a rich idea. Passion may dominate another that lacks precision of expression or rational ordering of ideas. When the value of a work can be so uneven, judgment is not an easy process.

One of the first questions the critic must ask is, What is art? Literary scholars have sometimes defined art, not by its adherence to a set of rules, but by more basic questions: What is the proper end of art? What are the characteristics of art? And what are the appropriate responses to art?

125

Another useful approach to judgment might be by using the classic formulation of the artistic process: the artist, the artifact, and the audience. Sayers has noted that art (especially literature) is a form of communication. It starts with an idea in the mind of the artist, takes shape as a work that lives independently of the artist, and is recreated through some mystical power in the mind and imagination of the reader, a person who may never have known the original artist.

Once we accept art as a means of communication, then we must ask the questions: What are the proper ends of art? What is appropriate to expect of the work of literature? What purposes can it, by its very nature, best serve? For the most part, we realize that the creative work is usually not the best vehicle for philosophy or polemic. The explicit preaching of theories or the detailed analysis of issues is usually better left to orators or essayists. Perhaps Hemingway expressed it best: "If you want to send a message, use Western Union."

Although this is generally a valuable piece of advice, it is one that some of the great writers have ignored. Camus and Dostoyevski and Shakespeare all have strong views, and all deal with great themes. They do it with considerable subtlety and within the confines of a form that lets the ideas evolve through characters and action. This is equally true of some of the more interesting of women's literature. George Eliot is rich with analytic responses to moral issues. But she finds a way to make those issues so important to the story that we remember the novel by its story as well as its theme.

For poetry or drama or short stories or novels, the merging of form and content must be so complete as to allow no simple moralistic paraphrase. Only someone as comic as James Thurber can get away with concluding each of his *Fables for Our Times*[90] with, "The Moral of this story is. . . ."

Good literature is rarely sermonizing. A politician may wax eloquent, hoping to move people to vote for or against a person or a bill in the legislature. Aside from that particular moment and purpose, his or her words may have no enduring value. Much of the polemic writing of the women's movement is likewise timebound, marked and limited by its purpose and period. It does not have the subtlety or the timelessness that we consider marks of great art. And good literature is rarely simply history or biography either. Though a literary biography may be the most accurate and detailed possible description of a life and literary career, it may also lack unity of theme or design or imagination. Such elements, so essential to art, are not necessarily a part of the "facts." Such writing may be clear and useful and interesting. And it may serve its purpose. But as a culture, we value as art that which transcends time, speaking to people in many eras, perennially relevant and moving.

A number of critics are inclined to express this quality of great art as *stasis*. Works of stasis are a delight in themselves, having no purpose other than adding beauty and wisdom to our lives. The reader contemplates such works and draws aesthetic delight from them, but she does not feel compelled to some action or idea as a result of having stepped into the created world of the artist. Polemic works, on the other hand, are *kinetic*. Their end is to push us or pull us to the support of this cause or that person. They tend to be specific in their purpose, limited in their scope. Those who espouse women's suffrage or prohibition or contraception or abortion or the rights of the fetus are all concerned with women's issues. They write prolifically, seeking both to act and to encourage others to act. Their words may cause actions we consider either good or evil, but they are rarely great art. In their zeal such authors seek to move the audience, an end usually incompatible with the nature of art.

Pornography is also kinetic in its intent. The pornographic writer seeks to arouse passions, to inflame the reader. The novel or film focuses on the scene of lust, not for its intrinsic value to the story and the development of character as a rule, but for the effect that it has on the reader or viewer. Violent action can have the same purpose—of producing an immediate effect rather than encouraging a more complete and complex form of human communication. Women's groups have become particularly concerned with the brutal tone of much pornographic literature that reduces women to victims and tools for pleasure.

Saying that pornography is not literature is not to suggest that literature is not full of love and sexuality. Forbidding their inclusions would be a foolish and useless admonition. Love is central to most lives. It gives most of our lives their core of meaning: love of God, of other people, of our husbands and children—these are life's great riches. Love, in all its complex

127

forms, is central to much of our greatest literature. And certainly women's literature has opened up a wider range of meaning for love than most of us had ever considered. Sexuality remains one of our most powerful motives for action during the major portion of our lives. The confusion of love and sex, the blending of it— these are common and powerful topics for literature. Yet in good writing, the sensuous or sensual scene is not described primarily to arouse the reader's passions. Rather, it is as an integral part of plot or character. Although sensuality can partially define one person, only a monster can be explained entirely by a single characteristic. No one is just a pretty face, and no one is simply an inflamed libido. Humans, created in the image of God, are more than collections of erogenous zones. Literature becomes pornography when sexuality dominates the story, when sex scenes are gratuitous, and when sexuality overshadows all other motives and definitions of people in an attempt to titillate the reader. This may describe a number of modern best sellers, but it certainly does not describe enduring art.

Art and Ideas

Because literature is so powerful a communicator, we must be concerned with what is being communicated. Not only does the artwork reflect the ideas of the artist, the controlling ideas of the form chosen, and the tastes of the audience for which it is intended, but it also reflects the world in which it is created. We need to become sensitive to the explicit and implicit ideas in the literature that we read.

Most of the novels we have studied in this book fall within the mind-set of the modern. They are therefore deeply marked with the overarching ideas of Charles Darwin, Karl Marx, and Sigmund Freud. Among them, these three taught the modern world that we are the offspring of apes, dominated by economic and sexual drives—hardly the beloved children of God, created in His image. This was bound to knock the lady off her pedestal and lift the slut from her gutter. Descendants of apes are not eligible for sainthood. Lascivious animals are not to be judged for the loss of virginity. Animals, after all, cannot get rid of their virginity fast enough, regardless of the partner involved.

Obviously the Christian reader finds herself swimming against these currents. She knows that she is more than an animal and that she has more complex drives than the simple need to couple. Her life is not simply a meaningless war against economic forces. The modern hedonistic trinity is no replacement for the Christian Trinity.

Modern philosophers and psychologists have been concerned with new means of discovering and defining self. Women, in particular, find themselves deeply involved in the process of learning about their true identity in a rapidly changing world. They seek the chance to live out their lives and to discover their identity in their choices rather than to rely on the codifications and stereotypes of the past. They do not want others to define them and their role. They want to find out for themselves by making attempts at a variety of things, by making mistakes and achieving successes. They seek liberation from many of the definitions and theories of the past.

This new freedom can be a problem to the Christian who does know that certain traditional truths cannot be so easily discarded. She cannot start with a blank tablet and then define herself. She does know that certain definitions are already in place: she is a child of God, she has His work to do, she is not her own person. She is not free in the modern sense because she has chosen to give her life to Christ, thereby achieving a still greater freedom in Him. She has her own proper work to do before she can find joy. Self is not central in her world; it has been replaced by God. So the Christian, male or female, cannot simply buy into modern secular presuppositions. The freedom to sell our lives for power, to pollute our marriages with adultery, to put ourselves before all others—these are not so different from Christ's choices in His great temptation. They are not marks of freedom, but invitations to enslavement. It is no liberation to break free of society's stereotypes and economic cages if we then turn to building our own new cages and stereotypes. Women have long been excluded, but we should not now choose to be included in every part of modern life and thought. We need to be selective in our choices, not following every banner raised in the cause of "Woman."

Such ideas are of special concern to the individual who reads with an eye to discovering the values implicit in literature. We can certainly appreciate the new sensitivity that we find in modern women's art. We can enjoy the enrichment of that art with imagery that we have not previously seen in literature. We now read more about sewing and cooking and household activities. We enjoy the increasing importance of small gestures, tiny events—the winning of little battles. We applaud the increased attention to the significance of every human being—not just the beautiful youth, but the aged arthritic, the pimply adolescent, or the tearful toddler as well.

Women have brought to literature a delight in the value of the gentle, nurturing spirit that loves idiosyncrasy and variety. The richness and paradox in language and in gesture are also a pleasure. Comic turns of phrase, fresh snatches of everyday life, new angles on old experience—these are all the riches available in the new women's literature.

But we would be wrong to applaud mindlessly. Not everything demands our unqualified admiration. We must remember that genius is rare in any age, among any people. Much of the writing of any era is hack work. Even in those rare cases where we spot genius, most of the ideas expressed in the beautiful form are either obvious or erroneous. Rarely does rich philosophy come clothed in perfect prose. And even when this, too, is present, we may find the work theologically unsound. A "perfect" writing is a pearl of great price. We must be discriminating judges.

We also should remember that the women's movement is not monolithic. In it are a vast number of people—men and women—who have many different concerns and attitudes. Some attend to economics, some language, some social change. Each question—whether about abortion or birth control or employment or religion—spawns violent and antithetical responses. Whether the speaker is conservative or liberal or somewhere in between, his or her attitudes have been formed by a lifetime of reading and experience and pressure. We must never forget the immense diversity of thought on women's issues.

There is no party line for the reader and writer to follow. Each issue must be considered on its own merits. Each work of art should be a separate inquiry. We need to experience it first as art, then judge it for its craft, and finally assess it for its assertions and presuppositions. No one is obliged to agree with every feminist artist or with every word of every work. Books are as various as the people who create them. We like some features and dislike others. We may disagree with one event or choice but still admire the general drift of the work or life. Some parts of some books we may applaud. Other portions of the same book may repel us.

Art mingles the acceptable and unacceptable as freely as does life. We all know people who speak in a variety of voices and perform in accordance with a variety of moral codes. We need not be blindly uncritical of either.

The plea, in short, is a simple one: be flexible and sensitive critics. And read the new literature about women for its life and insight.

For the modern Christian woman the response to the hedonistic trinity is the glorious Christian Trinity, each person of which carries meaning for the creative woman.

The Father is the loving parent who created woman in "our" image. Every woman who bears a child or breathes life into clay or brings forth a tasty and nourishing meal and sees that it is good knows something of the thrill of being a human reflection of this creative God.

In the person of the Son, women find a gentle man who refused to see His mother or any other woman as nothing but a woman. He challenged women to be His followers. He enjoyed their company, invited them to leave the kitchen. He talked theology with them. He did not turn from them if they were unclean or sinful. He looked them in the eye and helped them to find within themselves their own capacity for faith and for blessedness. He recommended to the men around Him that they accept the "feminine" virtues of gentleness and peace making. He even referred to God as a woman who had lost a coin and to Himself as a mother crying over her children. He was not afraid to be a servant who washed His disciples' feet and poured their wine. He was genuinely liberated, and in His image women have found the means to be all that they can be.

Jesus encouraged the men and women He met to go beyond tradition, to have life more abundantly. No simple conformist, no lazy, hazy thinker, Jesus challenged all whom He met. The old negative law of ritual righteousness thereby was transformed. We are to love God with all our hearts and minds and souls— with all our talents and emotions. And we are to love one another.

To assure us that we could be empowered to perform these actions, He promised us the strength of the Holy Spirit. From Genesis to Revelation, the Holy Spirit indwells women as well as men. Certainly the scene in the Upper Room makes this uncontrovertible. The women of the Christian church have shared fully all through the ages in the gifts of the Spirit. No other force has done more to provide mental and physical as well as spiritual liberation for millions of women. The Holy Spirit has made His home in our hearts, allowing us to find a liberation of spirit even when the world has tried to keep us hostage.

With such great guidance in our lives, we are fully equipped to be better critics, better women, and better citizens of God's kingdom. We have an obligation to live our lives with the full use of our talents, taking risks, growing, never settling into complacency. And we must seek out others who need to be encouraged or helped to let their lights shine clearly. This is one way that we can show our love for one another. If we are publishers, we should seek out new talent. If we are parents and teachers, we should encourage creative efforts. If we are students, we should express our delight in one another's success. We have no right to sneer or thwart or pervert God-given talents in ourselves or in others.

In short, literature is deeply embedded in us and our world. It reflects our deepest desires, our spoken ideas. We are not only the readers of literature and writers of it. We also are part of the environment in which literature is created. As Christians, we need to be aware that our enlightened responses can help create the conditions that nurture good literature. The incredible untapped abilities of women can increasingly flow into the mainstream of Western literature, satisfying the creative artists, delighting the creative readers, and enriching us all.

Glossary of Terms and Names Used in the Text

NOTE: Some of these books are available at your bookstore or library in a variety of fine editions, many in paperback. In such cases I have not furnished bibliographical detail.

Aeschylus: Greek writer of tragedies in the fifth century B.C. who created powerful female characters, including Clytemnestra.

Agnes of God: A contemporary American play about a nun. It was popular on Broadway in the early 1980s and later was made into a film.

Amazons: A band of female warriors described in ancient mythology. The term is used for a woman of stature and courage.

androgyny: The sharing of both masculine and feminine characteristics. The term is often used as an image of the totally human nature, both male and female.

Angelou, Maya: Author of a series of autobiographical books that describe the life of the black woman growing up in America. The first one, which describes her childhood, is the most famous and is entitled *I Know Why the Caged Bird Sings*.

Antigone: Daughter of Oedipus, heroine of a number of Greek plays. She refused to bend to the will of the monarch and conform to unjust law. She insisted on the burial of her brother. She died for her defiance.

Aphrodite: The Greek goddess of fleshly love, beauty, and fertility. She appears frequently in the Greek stories and reappears in Roman stories as Venus.

Apocrypha: Writings of dubious authenticity that have been considered Scripture by certain groups but have never been accepted as canon by the Jews or a majority of the Protestant churches. The term is also used to describe early Christian writings not included in the New Testament. A recent publication, *The Gnostic Gospels* (translated by Elaine Pagels [New York: Random House, 1979]), for example, describes Mary Magdalene as a love interest of Jesus and tells the story of His life from her point of view. For a brief description of these works, see Unger's *Bible Handbook*, "How the Bible Came to Us" (Chicago: Moody Press, 1967), pp. 882–94.

Aristotle (384–322 b.c.): Greek philosopher of considerable stature whose *Poetics* was to form the basis for much literary criticism and whose other works became central to Christian theology in the Middle Ages.

Ashtoreth: Another name for the Mother Goddess; the Hebrew term for Astarte.

Astarte: Phoenician goddess of fertility and sexual love and one of many names of the Mother Goddess—a figure worshiped by numerous cultures in the ancient world.

Athena: Greek goddess who was thought to have ruled over Athens, which was named for her. She loved wisdom and trickery, therefore relishing the activities of Odysseus. She was a virgin goddess who was a warrior in the style of the Amazons.

Augustine: A saint and early leader of the early-medieval church whose autobiographical *Confessions* is a powerful description of his conversion experience.

Austen, Jane: Early-nineteenth-century author whose novels describe domestic life in England. Among the best are *Pride and Prejudice* and *Emma*.

Babbitt: Character in a novel by Sinclair Lewis who epitomizes the dreary middle-class values of materialistic Americans of the 1920s.

Beatrice: A Florentine woman whom Dante knew and loved but did not marry. She became the image in his poetry and in his impressive three-part epic of the path from damnation to salvation, which he called *The Divine Comedy*.

Beauvoir, Simone de: Modern French philosopher, long-time companion of Jean Paul Sartre, the existentialist philosopher. Her book *The Second Sex* (New York: Bantam, 1970) was one of the earliest and most effectively reasoned of the modern studies of the woman in society and in thought.

Beowulf: Character in the Old English poem by the same name. He is an ideal type of warrior for the Anglo-Saxons: a wrestler and swimmer of enormous power.

bildungsroman: Type of novel popular in the late eighteenth and early nineteenth centuries that describes the coming of age of the young man, such as Dickens's *David Copperfield.*

Bombeck, Erma: Modern American syndicated columnist who amuses millions of men and women with anecdotes that are full of laughter at herself and her world.

Brontë, Charlotte: Nineteenth-century English novelist and sister of two other writers, Anne and Emily, and a brother, all of whom were imaginative and creative. Charlotte is best known for her novel *Jane Eyre,* which is the story of a young woman who becomes a governess and finds herself in the midst of complex emotional experiences. Emily Brontë wrote *Wuthering Heights,* capturing the emotional intensity of the limited lives of inhabitants of the English moors.

Browning, Elizabeth Barrett: Poet in the middle nineteenth century, wife of Robert Browning, and author of numerous excellent poems, many of which are collected in *Sonnets from the Portuguese.*

Bunyan, John: Seventeenth-century Christian writer who left us the powerful study of the Christian way in *Pilgrim's Progress.*

Byron, George Gordon (1788–1824): Lord Byron was a swash-buckling poet-adventurer who wrote of his own licit and illicit loves and his heroic ventures, such as swimming the Hellespont. He died young in Greece where he had gone to join the revolution for independence. Among his more memorable creations is the figure of Don Juan, a legendary figure whom Byron presented as a comic version of himself.

Cather, Willa: Twentieth-century American author whose stories and novels revolved around small towns in the Midwest and the farm people who lived there, often living simple and heroic lives. *My Antonia* and *O Pioneers!* are good examples of writing without mark of gender.

Chaucer, Geoffrey (1340–1400): English poet whose *Canterbury Tales* contain some of the best and most individualized portraits of women in medieval literature, in particular the Wife of Bath and the Prioress.

Chestnutt, Mary: A southern woman who lived through the Civil War and wrote of the events in *Diary from Dixie.*

Chopin, Kate: American writer at the end of the nineteenth century whose story *The Awakening* is considered one of the first of the modern feminist classics.

Clytemnestra: The powerful wife of Agamemnon, a character in Greek tragic drama who may have been modeled after a real historical figure. She takes a lover and plots to kill her husband while he is away at the Trojan War. Later her son and daughter plot to kill her in revenge for their father's murder.

Coleridge, Samuel Taylor (1772–1834): Romantic author whose criticism in *Biographia Literaria* was to become the basis for much modern thought, including the discussions of androgyny. His characterization of the Lamia figure in "Christabel" is a good example of the sinister beauty so appealing to the Romantics.

comic epic in prose: Term used by Henry Fielding in the preface to his novel *Joseph Andrews* as a way to describe the new novel.

Crane, Stephen: Turn-of-the-century American short-story writer and novelist who, in *The Red Badge of Courage,* described a young boy in the Civil War. In *Maggie: A Girl of the Streets* he described a young woman who became a prostitute because of social circumstances. "The Open Boat" is a particularly colorful picture of his naturalistic view of man against nature, a result of Darwinian views of man as animal and the later notion of the survival of the fittest.

Cybele: Lydian name for the Mother Goddess so popular in the ancient world.

Dante Alighieri: Medieval Italian writer whose *Divine Comedy* takes the path from earth through hell and purgatory to paradise. It is the most comprehensive poetic statement available to moderns of medieval Catholic religious and literary ideals, told in a thrilling but complex manner. This is one of the real masterpieces of Christian literature. The Dorothy L. Sayers translation contains notes that are especially rewarding to the Christian student.

Darwin, Charles (1809–1882): Nineteenth-century Englishman who described the process of evolution in his epoch-making volume *On the Origin of Species by Means of Natural Selection, or the Preservation of Favoured Races in the Struggle for Life* (1859).

Defoe, Daniel (1660–1731): Eighteenth-century English novelist and journalist who recognized women's need for education. His *Essay upon Projects* (1697) proposed an academy for women; his portrayal of the heroine in *Moll Flanders* is further testimony to his confidence that women are shrewd and fully capable of moral and immoral choices.

Delaney, Sheleigh: Modern British playwright who became famous with her play *A Taste of Honey.*

Diana: Roman goddess who was worshiped by the Ephesians—a deity of the moon, of the hunt, and of wild animals—probably another version of the Great Goddess of ancient myth.

Dickens, Charles: Nineteenth-century novelist whose books were enormously popular for their children and their sympathetic and emotional scenes. *Great Expectations, Oliver Twist,* and *David Copperfield* would serve as good examples of tales about the ignorant young boy who comes to understanding and maturity through a series of adventures.

Dickinson, Emily: A very special nineteenth-century New England writer who lived a quiet but intense life, produced some of the best lyric poems in American literature, and became a symbol of the reclusive poet.

Dionysus: The god of wine and inspiration in Greek mythology, the one to whom the plays were dedicated.

Don Juan: Legendary Spanish hero, used later by Byron as the restless womanizer and heartbreaker.

Dreiser, Theodore: Late-nineteenth-century and early-twentieth-century American novelist who, in *Sister Carrie* (1900), wrote of a young woman in a competitive, industrialized world, describing her frustrations and temptations.

Durant, Ariel and Will: Modern American authors of the massive series *The Story of Civilization.* Ariel was credited as coauthor only toward the end of their long partnership.

Electra: Mythical figure, the daughter of Agamemnon. She joined with her brother Orestes in plotting the murder of their mother, Clytemnestra. She was a heroine in several of the Greek dramas by Aeschylus, Sophocles, and Euripides.

Eliot, George (Mary Ann Evans) (1819–1880): Author of novels and works of criticism, including several books that describe her own life, notably *Adam Bede* and *The Mill on the Floss*. Moderns identify her as one of the first women novelists to reach out to a concern with moral and intellectual matters that are not confined by her sex.

Eliot, T. S.: Famous twentieth-century author whose literary criticism and poetry changed the face of modern literature. His long poem "The Wasteland" describes the disillusionment and faithlessness of the modern world in brilliant terms. A later poem, "The Four Quartets," was to describe the mystical experience that changed his life.

epic: A long narrative form that, in the days of Homer, was in poetry and presented with musical accompaniment. It is considered the ancestor of the modern comic, prose form of narrative, the novel.

Euripides: Last of the great Greek tragic dramatists (fifth century B.C.). Although a cynic about many things, including the immoral Greek gods, he was enormously sensitive to the problems of women. His plays *The Trojan Women* and *Medea* are particularly powerful examples of issues from the woman's point of view.

Faulkner, William: Modern American who through a series of short stories and novels has used the South as an image of the world. His particular sympathies with the downtrodden—the poor, the black, the helpless—make him an interesting example of a man who wrote about women in traditional ways but was capable of breaking through with new insights. Good examples of this would be *The Unvanquished; Go Down, Moses;* and *The Sound and the Fury*.

Fielding, Henry: Eighteenth-century novelist who wrote of young men full of lust and energy (*Tom Jones* and *Joseph Andrews*) and who also helped to shape and define the novel as an epic form.

Fitzgerald, F. Scott: Twentieth-century American fiction writer noted for his stories of talented and rich young flappers in the 1920s. Disturbed and disturbing female characters appear in such novels of his as *Tender Is the Night* and *The Great Gatsby*.

fortunate fall: Term critics sometimes use in describing the idea expressed in Milton's *Paradise Lost* of the blessing that came as a result of Adam's fall; i.e., that it prepared the way for the coming of Christ.

Freud, Sigmund: Nineteenth-century psychiatrist whose ideas on sexuality and hysteria were to change the world's understanding of human psychology. Subsequently, novelists portrayed characters as primarily motivated by sexuality, according to some critics, largely because of his work.

Friedan, Betty: Contemporary feminist whose book *The Feminine Mystique* was considered one of the most popular early statements regarding modern woman's dreary lot as housewife. In more recent days she has written more moderately of the need for home and family—and husband.

Gaskell, Elizabeth (1810–1865): English novelist who wrote *Life of Charlotte Brontë* (1857) and numerous works of social significance, some of them minor studies, such as *Cranford* (1853), and others on a wider scale, such as *North and South* (1855).

Gatsby: Flashy big spender and idealist about women in *The Great Gatsby* by Fitzgerald.

Gilman, Charlotte Perkins: Late nineteenth-century American writer and economist whose unorthodox life outraged many of her contemporaries. Her short story "The Yellow Wallpaper" is considered a classic study of the frustrated woman, smothered by love.

Glasgow, Ellen: Twentieth-century American author who was born in Richmond, Virginia, and who wrote about the South. Her autobiography, *The Woman Within,* is a picturesque study of the problems faced by the bright young southern lady. Other fictitious works, such as *Virginia, Vein of Iron,* and *Barren Ground,* are powerful studies of female characters faced with difficult choices.

Goldsmith, Oliver: Eighteenth-century British playwright, poet, and novelist whose *Vicar of Wakefield* was one of the most popular books of the century. The heroine, tricked by a wicked young rake, kills herself to teach him a lesson and to show how sorry she is for the error of her ways.

Gordon, Caroline: Twentieth-century American author who was a friend to most of the Fugitive Group at Vanderbilt and

A Voice of Her Own

who married Alan Tate for a time. Her criticism and her short stories are noted for their precision and their insights. "The Captive" is an unusual study of the woman-as-victim in a frontier setting.

Gothic novels: Popular style of novel from the late eighteenth century into the modern day, using ghosts, clanking chains, medieval castles, dungeons, and monsters, in which ghouls threaten innocent young maidens.

Great Mother: Otherwise known as the Mother Goddess, and as Ishtar, Venus, etc. This cult is chronicled in numerous books. An especially helpful example is *The Great Mother* by Erich Neumann (New York: Pantheon, 1955). The Hebrew fights with her are chronicled in a book called *The Hebrew Goddess,* by Raphael Patai (New York: Ktav, 1967). The cult of the Great Mother is clearly the source of much of the modern controversy about going "beyond God the Father" by such authors as Mary Daly.

Greer, Germaine: Contemporary British feminist who has written extensively about women, sexuality, and the arts. *The Obstacle Course* is a particularly helpful survey of the role of women (supposed or real) in the art world (painting and sculpture) over the ages. The parallels to literature are interesting.

Grendel and his mother: Characters in Beowulf, both of whom are monsters that threaten the mead hall, wrestle with Beowulf, and finally die at his hand.

Grimke sisters: Two nineteenth-century American sisters who became active in a number of political movements, including women's suffrage and the abolition of slavery.

Hammett, Dashiell: Twentieth-century American writer of detective fiction, including *The Maltese Falcon,* who was for years the housemate of Lillian Hellman but never her husband.

Hansberry, Lorraine: Twentieth-century playwright who wrote powerful stories, including at least one about the black experience in America that is among the best anywhere: *A Raisin in the Sun.*

Hardy, Thomas: Nineteenth-century British novelist and poet whose female characters, such as *Tess of the d'Urbervilles* (1891), are doomed for their beauty and sensitivity.

Harpy: Supernatural winged female creature in Greek and Roman mythology that has come to be the image of the vicious female.

Hawthorne, Nathaniel: One of the best and earliest of America's great Romantic writers. His *The Scarlet Letter* is frequently cited as an early example of a sensitive writer dealing with an issue crucial to women and to all humankind—the nature of guilt, of confession, and of redemption.

Hazzard, Shirley: Modern British woman who has written at least one excellent novel, *The Transit of Venus*, while pursuing her career with the United Nations.

Heilbroun, Carolyn: Modern American college professor and author who has written a number of detective stories, several books of criticism, and the classic study *Androgyny*.

Helen of Troy: Figure in ancient myth (both Greek and Roman) whose beauty was legendary. She was the purported cause of the Trojan War.

Hellman, Lillian: Modern American writer of plays, short stories, and commentary. Her memoirs are partially incorporated in such works as *An Unfinished Woman* and *Pentimento*. She has also written numerous political attacks on those she believed the enemies of Dashiell Hammett and herself. Her play about two young women starting a girls' school, *The Children's Hour*, was one of the first modern works hinting at lesbianism.

Hemingway, Ernest: Modern American novelist whose adventure stories and frequently violent novels chronicle a godless world in which man has only the refuge of love before he goes into that dark night of death. Hemingway is frequently powerful, as in *A Farewell to Arms, For Whom the Bell Tolls,* and *The Old Man and the Sea*.

Hera: Wife of the mythical Zeus, and his sister as well, jealous of his power, and probably another version of the Mother Goddess image.

Homer: Name given to the supposed creator of the ancient epics *The Iliad* and *The Odyssey,* who is pictured in literature as a blind bard, living about 850 B.C. The name, in fact, may be shorthand for a class of singers of epic songs.

Horace: Roman poet of the Silver Age of Rome whose odes summed up views of art and life. His satiric style became the mark of the classically educated man in the post-Renaissance world.

Ibsen, Henrik: Nineteenth-century playwright from Norway whose sympathy with women led him to create memorable characters, such as Hedda Gabler. *A Doll's House* was considered the beginning of modern drama and of modern feminist controversy on the stage. The image of the claustrophobic loving household which the mature woman must escape has become a standard part of the vocabulary of modern feminist discourse.

Irving, John: Contemporary American writer who won fame through his novel *The World According to Garp*. Others of his novels, such as *The Hotel New Hampshire*, also display great sensitivity to issues that involve women and a rejection of stereotyping by gender; but they are by no means Evangelical or Christian in their orientation.

Ishtar: Another name for the Great Goddess.

James, Alice: Sister of Henry and William James, the subject of an impressive study by Jean Strouse, who uses her as an example of the wasted and self-defeating nineteenth-century spinster.

Jong, Erica: Modern American whose first book, *Fear of Flying*, stayed on the best-seller list for some time but whose second book, *Fanny*, was more interesting as an example of a female version of the eighteenth-century picaresque novel. Her books follow the formula for contemporary best sellers; they are full of lust and adventure.

Keats, John (1795–1821): British Romantic poet of the early nineteenth century who generally pictured his ladies in dreamy, medieval forms. At least twice, in "Lamia" and "La Belle Dame Sans Merci," he used the sinister female that is a monstrous man-trap.

Kemble, Fanny: Nineteenth-century British actress who married a landed Philadelphia gentleman and soon found herself on a Georgia plantation. After she left the plantation and her husband and returned to England, she published her *Journal of Residence on a Georgia Plantation*, which describes in considerable detail the day-to-day life among the slaves.

Kerr, Jean: Contemporary American writer who has published some popular descriptions of the plight of the housewife among the children, including *Please Don't Eat the Daisies*.

Kingston, Maxine Hong: Contemporary Chinese-American writer whose novel *The Woman Warrior* is a fascinating study of alien attitudes toward the female.

"La Belle Dame Sans Merci": Keats's sinister image of the woman who threatens the young knight.

Lamia: A figure that combines an appearance of womanliness with a reality of reptilian nature. Such figures entwine the victim and suck his blood—a variation of the vampire image popular in Gothic literature.

Lessing, Doris: Contemporary writer of lengthy, meandering stories of women, particularly a group about Martha Quest. The one described in the text is *The Four-Gated City*.

Lost Generation: Term used for a group of talented young midwesterners who after World War I decided that they could not bear the middle-class values of America, so they went to live and love and drink and talk and write in Europe. Gertrude Stein was their mentor. The group included Hemingway and Fitzgerald.

Madonna: The Virgin Mary, a term used regarding her appearance with the Christ child in her arms in Christian art.

Madwoman in the Attic, The: A brilliant study (by Sandra Gilbert and Susan Gubar) of nineteenth-century women novelists as perceived by the "normal" world, who thought them quite mad.

Mailer, Norman: Fiercely masculine modern American novelist who frequently writes "advertisements" of himself and his activities. Early works included *The Naked and the Dead* and *The American Dream*. More recently he has engaged in some verbal battles with feminists that shed more heat than light.

Marx, Karl: Nineteenth-century philosopher and writer whose *Das Kapital* was to become the rallying point for the Communist Revolution.

Medea: Mythical Greek witch who saved and married Jason, the hero in search of the Golden Fleece. He later turned away from her to younger and more attractive possibilities, only to be met with the full fury of her anger and need for vengeance. Euripides tells her story sympathetically.

Medusa: Mythical Greek Gorgon figure with snaky hair and eyes that could paralyze threatening heroes. Eudora Welty uses her story as part of the imagery of *The Golden Apples.*

Melville, Herman: Nineteenth-century American author whose *Moby Dick* was to become a great American classic.

Michelangelo: Renaissance Italian painter and sculptor whose paintings for the ceiling of the Sistine Chapel continue to delight and intrigue modern travelers in Rome. The creation scene is particularly interesting, with the hand of God just touching that of Adam.

Mill, John Stuart: Nineteenth-century English philosopher whose book *The Subjection of Women* is an early example of sound reasoning about the plight of women. His marriage to an intelligent woman undoubtedly influenced his thinking on the subject.

Millett, Kate: Modern American whose dissertation on *Sexual Politics* was to become the basis for much of the discussion of sex as the basis for decision making and bullying.

Milton, John: Seventeenth-century English poet, one of the most powerful and clearly Christian poets of all time. The works noted in this book that impinge on the issue of women are *The Areopagitica* (which is a beautifully reasoned discussion of free speech), *Paradise Lost* (which is a poem of epic size and authority that chronicles the fall of mankind), and "Lycidas" (a pastoral poem that echoes Milton's own desire for fame as well as spiritual immortality).

Mitchell, Margaret: Twentieth-century American writer whose single claim to literary fame was the blockbuster of a novel and film, *Gone with the Wind.*

Morgan, Marabelle: Modern American who became incensed at the attack by Betty Friedan and others on traditional attitudes toward wives and mothers. She wrote *The Total Woman*—a response that infuriated the feminists.

Neumann, Erich: Author of *The Great Mother* and other works about psychology and archaeology. This particular work is a study of the female archetype.

O'Connor, Flannery: Brilliant twentieth-century southerner who described misfits of the South with an eye to their eternal souls. Her letters published posthumously under the title *The Habit of Being* are a moving testimony to her strength and her faith as she died full of joy with all the blessings of life.

Odysseus: Legendary hero of *The Odyssey*, the wily man who fought in the Trojan War and spent some ten years returning to his home and his wife.

Olsen, Tillie: Modern writer whose comments on exclusion appear in *Woman As Writer*, and who has also written a short essay entitled "As I Stand Ironing."

Pagels, Elaine: Modern American scholar who has translated and edited *The Gnostic Gospels*, including the Gospel According to Mary Magdalene.

pedagogical novel: Form of novel popular in the late eighteenth and early nineteenth centuries in both Europe and England that described the education of the young man or woman. Rousseau's *Emile* is a famous example of this form.

Pieta: The image of the crucified Christ on the lap of the mourning Virgin Mary, best known in the form sculpted by Michelangelo.

Plath, Sylvia: Modern American writer who wrote of her own experiences in *The Bell Jar* and chronicled her love-hate relationship with her father in "Daddy." Her poetry and short stories made her popular but could not keep her from the tragedy of an early suicide.

Provençal: Area in southern France that produced the flowering of medieval stories and songs known as romances. The code of chivalric love is usually associated with this region.

Rhinemaidens: The mythical ladies of the Rhine who caused the ships to wreck, much like the earlier sirens of Greek mythology had done.

Rich, Adrienne: Modern American poet and critic who has written an interesting book about her views on motherhood and feminism in *Of Woman Born*. She advocates lesbian love.

Richardson, Samuel: Eighteenth-century English novelist who wrote epistolary novels that had vulnerable and pure young women as their central characters. Both *Pamela* and *Clarissa* were enormously popular among the servants of the era, as well as among middle-class ladies.

romance: Term derived from the use of romance languages (i.e., rooted in Latin) that describes the stories developed in the late Middle Ages that told of ladies and their knights.

A Voice of Her Own

Rossetti, Christina: Nineteenth-century poet whose brothers were also poets and founders of the Pre-Raphaelite Brotherhood.

Sade, Marquis de: French author whose writing gave the term *sadism* to the infliction of pain upon a love object as a means of obtaining sexual release. His influence on the increasingly perverse views of love was enormous. See Mario Praz's book *The Romantic Agony* for a full description of the demonic hero, often associated with Byron.

Sand, George: Nineteenth-century French novelist and friend of Chopin. Her real name was Lucie Dudevant; she assumed the masculine name to allow her to write freely.

Sappho: Early Greek poet who wrote songs to the other women on the island where she apparently had her school, thus giving the name of the island (Lesbos) to female love (lesbianism).

Sayers, Dorothy L.: Modern British writer of detective fiction, plays, poetry, and polemics. Her translations of Dante's *Divine Comedy* and of the *Song of Roland* are still used in colleges for their notes as well as for the excellence of their language. Of her essays, *God the Creator,* "The Greatest Drama Ever Written," and *Are Women Human?* are among the most useful for a Christian perspective.

Scudéry, Mme. Magdeleine de: French novelist of the seventeenth century who wrote multivolume escapist novels. She represents the early female novelists who found a means of using the new form for fame and fortune.

Shelley, Mary: Wife of the poet and daughter of Mary Wollstonecraft, the political activist, she became the author of the famous *Frankenstein.*

siren: Mythical singer who sits on the rocks (near Greece) and lures the sailors to their death. Odysseus wanted to hear the songs but would not let his men listen, thus keeping them from wrecking the ship.

Sophia: Term used by Neumann and others for the lofty idealism that can come from dreaming of a lady.

Sophocles: Fifth-century B.C. dramatic artist who pictured a number of powerful women in his plays, including Antigone and Electra.

Spiller, Robert: Modern American literary critic whose famous book *The Cycle of American Literature* provides a useful pattern for analyzing an evolving literature.

Stanton, Elizabeth Cady: Nineteenth-century feminist whose edition of *The Woman's Bible* (1895) was an early effort at avoiding sexist language in Scripture.

Stein, Gertrude: Early-twentieth-century American expatriate whose salon in Paris attracted many of the bright young artists in the 1920s. Her autobiography is comically entitled *The Autobiography of Alice B. Toklas.*

Stein, Jean: Author of the briefly popular exposé about Edie Sedgwick, entitled *Edie.*

Thackeray, William Makepeace: Nineteenth-century British writer of enormous novels who created a memorable heroine, Becky Sharp (whose tongue matched her name), in *Vanity Fair.*

Thurber, James: The enormously funny writer for the *New Yorker* magazine who compiled a series of comic stories that he entitled *Fables for Our Times.*

vampire: A human bat who sucks human blood, the image of a Gothic sort of female given to draining men of their strength.

Venus: Roman goddess of love.

Walker, Alice: The contemporary southern writer who tells stories of black people in colorful speech. Her latest success is a book entitled *The Color Purple,* a book that is sensitive but not orthodox in its perspective.

Welty, Eudora: Modern American southern writer, a lady who continues to produce effective and feminine stories and novels that use the very special insights of the woman. Among her best are *Losing Battles* (discussed in the text) and *Delta Wedding.*

Wharton, Edith: Late-nineteenth-century and early-twentieth-century American realistic writer who spent the last thirty years of her life in France. Her novels about upper-middle-class men and women are brilliant studies in the moral issues of the day. I particularly recommend *The Age of Innocence* and *The House of Mirth,* which are discussed at some length in the book.

Whitman, Walt: Nineteenth-century American poet whose style was to change the pattern of American poetry.

Wollstonecraft, Mary: Mother of Mary Shelley and activist, along with her husband William Godwin, in numerous social causes. She was an early outspoken feminist.

Woolf, Virginia: Modern British writer whose extensive essays and novels and stories were to become central to the development of women's literature. Among the works cited at length in the text are *A Room of One's Own, The Common Reader, Mrs. Dalloway, To the Lighthouse,* and *The Voyage Out.*

Wright, Richard: Modern American author of stories and novels about the black experience in America, including *Black Boy,* and *Native Son.*

References

[1] Tillie Olsen, "As I Stand Ironing," in *Woman As Writer,* ed. Jannette Webber and Joan Grumman (Boston, Mass.: Houghton Mifflin, 1979).

[2] Ellen Glasgow, *The Woman Within* (New York: Harcourt, Brace, 1954); *Virginia* (Garden City, N.Y.: Doubleday, 1913); *Vein of Iron* (New York: Harcourt, Brace, 1935); *Barren Ground* (Gloucester, Mass.: Peter Smith, 1973).

[3] Josef Peiper, *Leisure: The Basis of a Culture* (New York: New American Library, 1981).

[4] Dorothy L. Sayers, *Divine Comedy* (New York: Penguin, 1949). *Song of Roland* (New York: Penguin, 1957). *Creed and Chaos?* "The Greatest Drama Ever Told" (New York: Harcourt, Brace, 1949). *Are Women Human?* (Grand Rapids: Eerdmans, 1971).

[5] Dorothy L. Sayers' series featuring Lord Peter Wimsey began with *Whose Body?* and continued through *In the Teeth of Evidence* (London: Victor Gallancz Ltd., 1923–1972).

[6] Dorothy L. Sayers, trans., *The Divine Comedy* and *Song of Roland;* also *Hell* (New York: Penguin, 1950), *Purgatory* (New York: Penguin, 1956), and *Paradise* (New York: Penguin, 1962).

[7] Virginia Woolf, *A Room of One's Own* (San Diego: Harcourt Brace Jovanovich, 1981); *To the Lighthouse* (San Diego: Harcourt Brace Jovanovich, 1964); *The Voyage Out* (San Diego: Harcourt Brace Jovanovich, 1968); *Mrs. Dalloway* (San Diego: Harcourt Brace Jovanovich, 1964); *The Common Reader* (New York: Harcourt Brace Jovanovich, 1925).

[8] Woolf, *A Room of One's Own,* p. 74.

[9] Robert Spiller, *The Cycle of American Literature* (New York: Free Press, 1967).

[10] Fanny Kemble, *Journal of Residence on a Georgia Plantation* (Athens, Ga.: University of Georgia Press, 1984).

[11] Mary Chestnutt, *Diary from Dixie* (Cambridge, Mass.: Harvard University Press, 1980).

[12] Lillian Hellman, *An Unfinished Woman* (New York: Bantam, 1979). *Pentimento: A Book of Portraits* (Boston: Little, Brown, 1974). *The Children's Hour* (New York: Bobbs-Merrill, 1972).

[13] Maya Angelou, *I Know Why the Caged Bird Sings* (New York: Random, 1970).

[14] Simone de Beauvoir, *The Second Sex* (New York: Bantam, 1970).

[15] Betty Friedan, *The Feminine Mystique* (New York: Norton, 1963).

[16] Marabelle Morgan, *The Total Woman* (Old Tappan, N.J.: Revell, 1975).

[17] Betty Friedan, *The Second Stage* (New York: Summit, 1981); and *It Changed My Life* (New York: Putnam, 1977).

[18] See n. 7 and Virginia Woolf, *The Second Common Reader* (New York: Harcourt, Brace & World, 1932).

[19] Christina Rossetti was a nineteenth-century poet whose brothers were also poets and founders of the Pre-Raphaelite Brotherhood.

[20] Kate Millett, *Sexual Politics* (Garden City, N.Y.: Doubleday, 1970).

[21] Samuel Richardson, *Clarissa* (New York: Modern, 1950); idem, *Pamela* (New York: Dutton, 1962).

[22] Daniel Defoe, *Moll Flanders* (New York: Penguin, 1978). William Hazlitt, ed., *The Works of Daniel Defoe, With a Memoir of His Life and Writings* (London: J. Clements, 1840–1843).

[23] Henry Fielding, *Tom Jones* (New York: Random, 1950).

[24] Charlotte Brontë, *Jane Eyre* (New York: Bantam, 1981).

[25] Erica Jong, *Fear of Flying* (New York: Harper & Row, 1973); idem, *Fanny* (Boston: New American Library, 1980, 1981).

[26] Dorothy L. Sayers explored this concept in her lively book on creativity, *The Mind of the Maker* (New York: Harper & Row, 1979).

[27] See Acts 19:24–35.

[28] A good source to further understand the origins of the pagan "Earth Mother" myths is Erich Neumann's *The Great Mother* (New York: Pantheon, 1955).

[29] The tortured lives of Hart Crane, Dylan Thomas, and Tennessee Williams demonstrate the need for frenzy.

[30] Elizabeth Cady Stanton, *The Woman's Bible* (Seattle: Coalition of Women and Religion, 1974).

[31] A premier doctrine of the Reformation, but one often overlooked in our theological literature is the doctrine of the priesthood of every believer. The obvious implication is that God has ordained that every believer has ministry functions regardless of gender. Not many have the gifts of public teaching and ministry; but no one is ruled out of these by gender.

[32] Sappho was the early Greek poetess who wrote songs to the other women on the island where she apparently had her school, thus giving the name of the island (Lesbos) to female love (lesbianism).

[33] The German nun Hroswitha is said to have written hymns, Latin plays, and biographies of saints' lives.

[34] *The Obstacle Course: The Fortunes of Women Painters and Their Work* (New York: Farrar, Straus and Giroux, 1979).

[35] Woolf, *A Room of One's Own*, p. 74.

[36] Marie Hong Kingston, *The Woman Warrior: Memoirs of a Girlhood Among Ghosts* (New York: Knopf, 1976).

[37] Mary Wollstonecraft wrote *A Vindication of the Rights of Women* (1792).

[38] In his poem "When I Consider How My Light Is Spent."

[39] Others include the Brontë sisters, Emily Dickinson, and Elizabeth Gaskell (see glossary).

[40] Sylvia Plath, *The Bell Jar* (New York: Harper & Row, 1971). See also idem, *Ariel* (New York: Harper & Row, 1965).

[41] Sandra M. Gilbert and Susan Giubar, *The Madwoman in the Attic: A Study of Women & the Literary Imagination in the Nineteenth Century* (New Haven: Yale University Press, 1979).

[42] Edith Wharton, *The Age of Innocence* (New York: Scribner, 1983); idem, *The House of Mirth* (New York: Berkley, 1981).

[43] See, for example, the new evangelical work by Ronald and Beverly Allen, *Liberated Traditionalism: Men and Women in Balance* (Portland: Multnomah, 1985).

[44] Carolyn G. Heilbroun, *Toward a Recognition of Androgyny* (New York: Norton, 1982).

[45] See note 22.

[46] John Stuart Mill, *The Subjection of Women* (Arlington Heights, Va.: Davidson, 1980).

[47] Henrik Ibsen, *The Doll's House & Other Plays* (New York: Penguin, 1965).

[48] The German nun Hroswitha who copied the plays of Terence.

[49] Mme. de Scudéry was a French novelist of the seventeenth century who wrote multivolume escapist novels. She represents the early female novelists, who found a means of using the new form for fame and fortune.

[50] George Eliot (Mary Anne Evans), *Adam Bede* (New York: Penguin, 1980); see also *The Mill on the Floss* (New York: Airmont, 1964).

[51] Emily Dickinson, a very special nineteenth-century New England writer, who lived a quiet but intense life, produced some of the best lyric poems in American literature, and became a symbol of the reclusive poet.

[52] Sheleigh Delaney, *A Taste of Honey* (New York: Grove, 1959).

[53] Alice Walker, *The Color Purple* (San Diego: Harcourt Brace Jovanovich, 1982). Flannery O'Connor, *The Habit of Being* (New York: Farrar, Straus and Giroux, 1979).

[54] Jean Stein, *Edie: An American Biography* (New York: Knopf, 1982).

[55] Gertrude Stein, *The Autobiography of Alice B. Toklas* (New York: Random, 1960).

[56] Charlotte Perkins Gilman, "The Yellow Wallpaper" in *About Women: A Collection of Short Stories*, ed. Helen Reed (New York: World, 1943).

[57] Sylvia Plath, *The Journals of Sylvia Plath* (New York: Dial, 1982). See also Aurelia Schobre Plath, ed., *Letters Home* (New York: Harper & Row, 1975).

[58] Unfortunately this sort of attitude pervades some of the more radical feminists and pantheistic environmentalists who share a loathing of Christianity in particular and Western tradition in general (which is largely based on the Judeo-Christian world view).

[59] On the connection of Jezebel with the worship of Ishtar, see 1 Kings 16:31–33; 18:19; 19:1–2.

[60] Erich Neumann, *The Great Mother: An Analysis of the Archetype* (Princeton, N.J.: Princeton University Press, 1964).

[61] Examples of such fairy tales are *Snow White* and *Cinderella*.

[62] Euripides, *Medea*. Contained in *Loeb Classical Library*, vol. 4 (Cambridge, Mass.: Harvard University Press; London: William Heinemann, Ltd., 1964).

[63] Clytemnestra and Electra appear in Aeschylus' *Orestia* (525–456 B.C.). Electra and Antigone appear in plays by those names by Sophocles (496–406 B.C.).

[64] See notes in Dante Alighieri, *Purgatorio*, vol. 2 of *The Divine Comedy*, trans. Dorothy L. Sayers, 3 vols. (New York: Penguin, 1955).

[65] William Makepeace Thackeray, *Vanity Fair* (New York: Dodd, Mead, 1943).

[66] Oliver Goldsmith, *The Vicar of Wakefield* (London: Oxford University Press, 1929).

[67] John Pielmeier, *Agnes of God*. See Otis L. Guernsey, Jr., ed., *Theater Yearbook: The Best Plays of 1981–82* (New York: Dodd, Mead, 1983).

[68] T. S. Eliot, "The Wasteland," in *T. S. Eliot*, ed. Joachim Seyppel (New York: Unger, 1972).

[69] John Keats, "Lamia" and *"La Belle Dame sans Merci,"* in *"Lamia," A Book of English Literature*, ed. Franklyn Bliss Snyders and Robert Grant Martin (New York: Macmillan, 1933).

[70] Samuel Taylor Coleridge, "Christabel," in *Poems of Samuel Taylor Coleridge*, ed. Babette Deutsch (New York: Crowell, 1967).

[71] See F. Scott Fitzgerald, *The Great Gatsby* (New York: Scribner, 1925).

[72] John Keats, "The Grecian Urn," in *The Selected Poetry of Keats*, ed. Paul deMan (New York: Signet Classics, 1966).

[73] Kate Chopin, *The Awakening* (New York: Gordon, 1974).

[74] Numbers 12:1–16.

[75] The frenzied female worshipers appear in the *Bacchae* by Euripides as well as in much Greek art.

[76] The Gnostic Gospels depict Mary Magdalene as a love interest. These Gospels have never been accepted as inspired by the church fathers. There are several rigid standards used to determine the authenticity and inspiration of the books included in the Bible. The books excluded from the Bible (noncanonical books) were denied canonical status for a variety of reasons: some were outright forgeries attributed to various disciples of Christ; others were imaginative constructions of facts and fiction with no evidence of divine inspiration; still others were preposterous and inconsistent with the character of canonical works. For a brief description of these works, see *Unger's Bible Handbook*, "How the Bible Came to Us" (Chicago: Moody Press, 1967), pp. 882–94.

[77] A battle fought in England through the middle years of the nineteenth century. The act passed in 1882. Discussed on page 180 of *The Norton Anthology of Literature by Women* by Sandra M. Gilbert and Susan Gubar (New York: Norton, 1985).

[78] Lily Bart is a character in Edith Wharton's novel *The House of Mirth* (1905).

[79] Sylvia Plath, "Daddy," in *Ariel*.

[80] Comic epic in prose was a term used by Fielding in the preface to his novel *Joseph Andrews* as a way to describe the new novel.

[81] Representative works are: Theodore Dreiser, *Sister Carrie;* Frank Norris, *The Octopus;* Stephen Crane, *Maggie—A Girl of the Streets* and *The Open Boat.*

[82] Shirley Hazzard, *The Transit of Venus* (New York: Berkley, 1981).

[83] George Noel Gordon, *Lord Byron* (1788–1824), swam the Hellespont to reenact the mythological feat of Leander. According to Greek myth, Leander, who lived in Abydus, swam the Hellespont each night to be with Hero. She lived in the town of Sestos. One night Leander lost his way when a storm blew out the blazing torchlight on the other side. He drowned. Byron's duplication of Leander's nightly swim is recorded in his poem, "Written After Swimming from Sestos to Abydos." Lord Byron, contained in *The Complete Poetical Works of Byron,* Cambridge ed. (Cambridge, Mass.: Riverside, 1933).

[84] Doris Lessing's *Four-Gated City* (New York: Knopf, 1969) is a part of this series.

[85] The "fortunate fall" is a term critics sometimes use in describing the idea expressed in Milton's *Paradise Lost* of the blessing that came as a result of Adam's fall; i.e., that it prepared the way for the coming of Christ.

[86] Arthur Laurents wrote the play *The Turning Point.* See Leslie Halliwell, *Halliwell's Film and Video Guide* (New York: Scribner, 1983).

[87] Norman Mailer, *The Naked and the Dead* (New York: Harper & Row, 1980).

[88] John Irving, *The World According to Garp* (New York: Dutton, 1978).

[89] Adrienne Rich. *Of Woman Born* (New York: Norton, 1976).

[90] James Thurber, *Fables for Our Times* (New York: Harper & Row, 1952).

For Further Reading

The books cited throughout the text and mentioned in the references (with bibliographic data) provide the reader with a thorough survey of the best of women's literature. Besides those, the following titles are recommended by the editors.

Women's Literature

Gilbert, Sandra M., and Gubar, Susan, eds. **The Norton Anthology of Literature by Women: The Tradition in English.** New York: W. W. Norton, 1985.

This work represents the best women writers over the past two millennia, featuring more than 150 authors from dozens of different countries. It will likely be the standard text in courses on women's literature and women's studies for the next several years. It should teach women that writing is not a foreign exercise for females and that writing may exhibit excellence. The text does exhibit some weaknesses, including short essays that are not representative of their authors' best efforts, and the commentary by the editors is uneven.

Sayers, Dorothy. **The Mind of the Maker.** New York: Harper & Row, 1979.

A leading British author brilliantly discusses a variety of theological themes. Her purpose is to tantalize the reader with a refreshing attitude toward God and Christian thought.

———. **Are Women Human?** Grand Rapids: Eerdmans, 1971.

Sayers' essay has become a standard work that is recognized as legitimate criticism of the church's treatment of women. She argues that the church has failed to treat women as well as Christ did.

Christian Views of Women's Issues

Allen, Ronald, and Allen, Beverly. **Liberated Traditionalism.** Portland: Multnomah, 1985.

A recent Evangelical work attempting to evaluate the women's movement. The authors formulate a response to feminism that remains sensitive to women's needs and yet adheres to an orthodox view of biblical authority.

Clark, Stephen B. **Man and Woman in Christ.** Ann Arbor: Servant, 1980.

A comprehensive work that deals with sociological and psychological aspects of women's issues. Scholarly and conservative in approach.

A Voice of Her Own

DeJong, Peter, and Wilson, Donald R. **Husband and Wife: The Sexes in Scripture and Society.** Grand Rapids: Zondervan, 1979.

In this work, a Christian sociologist examines biological, social-scientific, and biblical evidence about the roles of men and women in the home and society. The author successfully integrates the three approaches to construct a thoughtful Christian perspective on the changing roles of women and men.

Foh, Susan T. **Women and the Word of God.** Grand Rapids: Baker, 1979.

A Reformed approach that deals mainly with the biblical passages that discuss women. The work stresses scholarly exegesis of the biblical text, adheres to biblical authority, and takes a moderate-to-conservative stance on the issues.

Hurley, James B. **Man and Woman in Biblical Perspective.** Grand Rapids: Zondervan, 1981.

Hurley examines ancient cultures and biblical backgrounds in order to discuss women's issues. Best source for the discussion of the veiling of women and other such practices found in the biblical text. This work also emphasizes the exegesis of biblical texts about women. Moderate in approach.

Tischler, Nancy. **Legacy of Eve.** Atlanta: John Knox, 1977.

This work gives a concise look at biblical portrayals of women—from Eve to Sarah to Mary and on to the women of Revelation (harlot, mother, and bride). It deals with biblical data on the single woman, woman as temptress, and woman as sovereign. Relating scriptural patterns to human history, the book explores the universal qualities of women and their meaning for women today.

_____. **Dorothy L. Sayers: The Pilgrim Soul.** Atlanta: John Knox, 1980.

This biography amply demonstrates how Sayers chose to live as "a saint in the world not in the cloister." It documents the obstacles overcome by Sayers, taking us beyond the mystery writer to glimpses of the author as dramatist, essayist, and scholar. Portrayals of her personal spiritual journey and her faithfulness in a troubled marriage give us a fully human portrait of this remarkable woman.

Williams, Don. **The Apostle Paul and Women in the Church.** Van Nuys: BIM, 1977.

A thorough look at the Pauline writings about women, with commentary on every text where Paul discusses women. The author comes to fair conclusions, and the reader is treated to a realistic view of Paul's theological view of women. This work successfully cuts through much of the confusion over Paul's views.

Index

POP CULTURE BIOS

EMMA
STONE

STAR OF THE STAGE, TV, AND FILM

HEATHER E. SCHWARTZ

 Lerner Publications Company

MINNEAPOLIS

To my glam grandma,
Grace Kanner

Lerner Publications Company
A division of Lerner Publishing Group, Inc.
241 First Avenue North
Minneapolis, MN 55401 U.S.A.

For reading levels and more information, look up this title at
www.lernerbooks.com.

Library of Congress Cataloging-in-Publication Data

Schwartz, Heather E.
    Emma Stone : star of the stage, tv, and film / by Heather E.
Schwartz.
       p.   cm. — (Pop culture bios)
    Includes index.
    ISBN 978-1-4677-1440-2 (lib. bdg. : alk. paper)
    ISBN 978-1-4677-2498-2 (eBook)
    1. Stone, Emma, 1988- Juvenile literature. 2. Actors—
United States—Biography—Juvenile literature. 3. Singers—
United States—Biography—Juvenile literature. I. Title.
PN2287.S73S385 2014
791.4302'8092—dc23
[B]   2013013633

Manufactured in the United States of America
1 – PC – 12/31/13

INTRODUCTION

All her life, Emma Stone wanted to host the comedy show *Saturday Night Live*. In 2010, the young actress learned she was about to get her chance. So what did she do? Nope, she didn't jump up and down with excitement. She burst into tears.

But she wasn't upset—not at all. She was just overcome with emotion. She wondered if she'd recover in time to actually do the job.

She dialed up her friend Justin Timberlake (yes, *that* Justin Timberlake!), who'd hosted before. His advice: if she was going to cry on the show, fine—as long as she made it funny.

As it turned out, Emma didn't cry. She cracked up the audience, using stories from her own life to kick off the jokes.

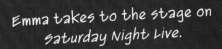
Emma takes to the stage on Saturday Night Live.

"I've wanted to be on this stage since I was a little girl. That's why when I was 14, I convinced my parents to let me move to L.A. to pursue acting," she said during her opening monologue. "A few years later I was doing movies and a few years after that I'm here hosting *Saturday Night Live*. And it is truly a dream come true."

MONOLOGUE =
a solo speaking performance

Emma loved doing the skits for Saturday Night Live.

CHAPTER ONE

GIRL WITH A GOAL

Emma's hometown of Scottsdale, Arizona (ABOVE),
is next to Arizona's capital, Phoenix.

Emma is one girl who knows how to get what she wants. It all started when she was growing up in Scottsdale, Arizona. Emily Jean (that's her real name!) was born on November 6, 1988. As a kid, she was noisy and bossy. Her role models? Loud, funny, famous guys, like Steve Martin and John Candy. She loved their movies and wanted to be just like them.

There was one hitch, though. When Emma was eight, she started having panic attacks. Out of nowhere, she'd suddenly be slammed with feelings of fear.

FAMILY MATTERS

Emma has one younger brother, Spencer (LEFT). She once took him as her date to an award ceremony. He made her promise to talk about him in her acceptance speech. She got lots of laughs when she did.

As a kid, Emma loved computers. She even designed her own websites! She also loved writing. So she started an online magazine for girls. If she hadn't become an actor, she would've wanted to be a web designer or a journalist.

During the school day, she just wanted to go home. After school, she was scared to go to friends' houses to play. She didn't feel strong or confident. She felt sick. How was she supposed to become a famous funny girl?

Therapy helped, and so did acting. Emma liked getting onstage and making people laugh. It made her feel good. Soon Emma started believing in herself again. She was back to dreaming big. Sure, at first glance, she might not *look* like star material.

FUNNY GIRL

The first movie Emma remembers watching is *The Jerk*, starring Steve Martin (LEFT). It made her want to do comedy.

AUDITIONS =
tryouts for parts in
movies, shows, or plays

She wore glasses
and braces. She still
sucked her thumb. But
so what? She wasn't
about to let anything
get in her way.

Emma wore braces
in sixth grade.

The Acting Bug

Emma acted at a local youth theater. She also performed
in their comedy improv group. By the time she was twelve,
she was serious about acting. In fact, she wanted to leave
school to make more time for auditions. Most parents
probably wouldn't go for
that plan. And most kids
wouldn't have the guts to
ask. But Emma made sure
her mom and dad heard
her out.

IMPROV =
short for improvisation,
which means "to act by
making up lines on the spot"

She made a presentation on foam boards and convinced her parents to homeschool her.

The same year, Emma flew to Hollywood, in Los Angeles, to audition for a role on a Nickelodeon show. She didn't get the part. But she did learn one important lesson: This crazy city wasn't for her. She did *not* want to live in L.A.

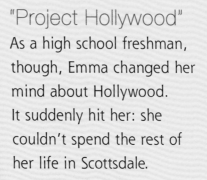

"Project Hollywood"

As a high school freshman, though, Emma changed her mind about Hollywood. It suddenly hit her: she couldn't spend the rest of her life in Scottsdale.

MAKING STUFF UP

Emma loved working on *The House Bunny* and *Superbad*—two films she later acted in—because she got to do improv in many of her scenes.

Emma decided in high school that she wanted to move out of her hometown.

Sure, she'd been in tons of local theater productions. But now she was ready to aim for the silver screen. And her hometown wasn't exactly Moviemaking Central. If she wanted a shot at a film career, she would *have* to move to L.A. And she would have to convince her parents it was the right thing to do.

So she created another presentation. After all, it had worked before! This time, she went high-tech. She used PowerPoint and added music—Madonna's song "Hollywood," of course! The finished product was called "Project Hollywood." She showed it to her parents and served them popcorn while they watched. The result: at the age of fifteen, Emma left home for Los Angeles.

Emma's mom (LEFT) headed to L.A. with the young actress to help Emma follow her dreams.

CHAPTER TWO

BREAKING IN

Emma has been both blonde (LEFT) and brunette (RIGHT).

In 2004, Emma and her mom, Krista, moved into an apartment in L.A. For eight months, Emma tried out for roles. For eight months, she got rejected.

It was enough to make any girl feel as though she had a great big *L* stuck to her forehead. But when Emma couldn't take it anymore, she didn't quit. Instead, she made a bold change. The problem had nothing to do with her talents, she decided. The problem was her hair.

RUFF START

Before she made it as a movie star, Emma worked part-time baking treats for dogs. She says she wasn't very good at it, though!

Dyeing for a Break

As a natural blonde, Emma often ended up auditioning for cheerleader roles. But she wasn't getting those parts. So she decided to try something new. She dyed her long locks dark brown. Maybe *that* would help.

Emma's husky voice sets her apart from other actresses. But do you know how she got it? As a baby, she cried a *lot*. She screamed so much that she damaged her vocal cords!

Soon after, Emma's mom found out about a VH1 reality show. It was actually a talent competition. Actors and actresses would compete for roles on a planned sitcom called *The New Partridge Family*—a reboot of a popular 1970s show. In the original show, the teenage character Laurie Partridge had brown hair. With her brand-new dye job, Emma had just the right look for that role.

Of course, looks aren't everything, even in Hollywood. The contestants were judged as actors and singers too. That's where Emma showed her true talents. She nailed her cover of Pat Benatar's "We Belong"—and won the competition!

COVER =
a performance of a song originally written and sung by someone else

Super Score

The New Partridge Family wasn't a hit. In fact, the show was canceled before it even aired. Emma must've been bummed. Or was she? By then, she was tight with the show's music producer. Through him, she met her lawyer. And through her lawyer, she met her manager, Doug Wald. Now she had a pro on her side. Doug could help her build a solid acting career.

> MANAGER =
> a person who helps guide an actor's career

First, she started getting roles on TV. She appeared on *Malcolm in the Middle* and the FOX show *Drive*.

Emma played a young driver in cross-country road races on the FOX show *Drive*.

Emma, shown here on set with Jonah Hill (LEFT), got a lot of laughs in her first movie, Superbad.

But it wasn't all easy breezy from then on. When Emma went for a major role on the NBC show *Heroes*, actress Hayden Panettiere beat her out.

That was a low point for Emma. But soon, she scored an even better part: the role of Jules in the movie *Superbad*.

NAME GAME

Emma started her acting career as Emily Stone. She switched to Riley Stone for a while. Finally, she decided to go with Emma, her mother's nickname for her.

Superbad was a huge hit. And Emma's comedic timing and natural beauty got a lot of attention.

But that was just the beginning. Between 2008 and 2009, she was in five more movies: *The Rocker*, *The House Bunny*, *Ghosts of Girlfriends Past*, *Zombieland*, and *Paper Man*. In 2010, she landed her first lead role, in the movie *Easy A*.

In *Easy A*, Emma narrated the story with video blogs and funny posters.

Emma glams up for the 2011
Golden Globe Awards.

CHAPTER THREE

LEADING LADY

Emma and Andrew Garfield (LEFT) try to
keep their love on the down low.

One morning in late 2010, Emma's phone woke her out of a deep sleep. The caller was Doug Wald, her manager. Emma was afraid that something horrible had happened. Why else would he call at 5:30 a.m.?

Actually, Doug had amazing news to share. Emma's star turn in *Easy A* had been a big hit. She'd been nominated for a Golden Globe Award!

Emma was officially a superstar on the rise. In 2011, she starred in two more movies, *The Help* and *Crazy, Stupid, Love*. The same year, she was cast as Gwen Stacy, the female lead in *The Amazing Spider-Man*.

Emma + Andrew = <3

On the set of *The Amazing Spider-Man*, Emma had great chemistry with costar Andrew Garfield.

AND THE WINNER IS...

Emma didn't win the Golden Globe for her performance in *Easy A*. But she did win an MTV Movie Award for Best Comedic Performance.

PAPARAZZI =
<u>photographers who follow celebrities
without their permission</u>

Soon their on-screen romance became a real-life love story. For a while, they tried to keep it a secret. Even though they were both famous, they still wanted their privacy. When reporters asked, Emma told them she just didn't want to talk about her personal life.

But Emma and her new bf couldn't hide from the paparazzi when they went out together. So one afternoon, they decided to take advantage of the unwanted attention. When photographers followed them to take pictures, the couple held up signs. Their message directed people to websites for charitable organizations. One was Gilda's

DOG DAYS

Over the holidays in 2012, Emma and Andrew adopted a dog together. They rescued their golden retriever, Ren, from a shelter.

Emma and Andrew take Ren for a stroll.

WE JUST FOUND OUT
THAT THERE ARE PAPARAZZI
OUTSIDE THE RESTAURANT
WE WERE EATING IN,
SO...WHY NOT TAKE THIS →

OPPORTUNITY TO BRING
ATTENTION TO ORGANIZATIONS
THAT NEED AND DESERVE IT?
WWW. WWO. ORG
WWW. GILDASCLUBNYC.ORG
Have a great day!

Emma and Andrew decided to mix
it up with the paparazzi.

Club, a support network for people living with cancer.
It was named after Gilda Radner, a comedian Emma
admired, who died of the disease.

Celeb-rating a Good Cause

Promoting a website for
cancer survivors wasn't a
random choice for Emma.
Her mom is a breast cancer
survivor. As a celebrity,
Emma could use her fame
to support a cause she really
believed in.

EMMA'S FAVS

Actress: Diane Keaton
Band: the Beatles
Book: *Franny and Zooey* by
       J. D. Salinger
Food: oysters
Movie: *City Lights*

In 2012, Emma and her mother posed together in a Revlon ad for breast cancer awareness. Emma was interviewed about it, and on this topic, she didn't hold back. She told reporters that when her mother was declared cancer-free, she and her mom got matching tattoos to celebrate.

As Emma explained, their shared tattoo is a small picture of blackbird feet. It stands for the Beatles song "Blackbird," which is about turning negatives into positives. The tattoo was actually drawn by former Beatle Sir Paul McCartney. Emma had met Sir Paul through her *Zombieland* costar Woody Harrelson. Later, she'd written Sir Paul a letter asking him to make the design. Anything for Emma!

Emma shows off her wrist tattoo.

Paul McCartney was the one celebrity Emma had always wanted to meet. So when she was invited to dinner at his house, she was starstruck! But she loosened up when she and the other guests played party games with their host.

All-Around "It" Girl

Eight years after moving to L.A., Emma was everywhere. She walked the red carpet at the Oscars. She appeared on magazine covers and in ads—not to mention all the movies she made. She joined the star-studded cast of *Gangster Squad*.

Emma starred alongside Ryan Gosling (RIGHT) for the 1940s-era film *Gangster Squad*.

She reprised her role as Gwen Stacy in *The Amazing Spider-Man 2*. She even took the part of a cartoon character, voicing Eep in *The Croods*.

Emma loves acting, of course. But that doesn't mean she has a one-track mind. She bakes to help herself relax.

REPRISE = *a repeat appearance*

FAMOUS FRIENDS

Many of Emma's gal pals are as famous as she is. She's tight with singer Taylor Swift (LEFT) and actress Jennifer Lawrence.

Emma hates going to the gym, so she finds other ways to stay fit. Her favs: swimming, rock climbing, pilates (special muscle exercises), and walking.

She loves reading—when she can find the time. She even got into biology when she visited a lab to prepare for her role in *The Amazing Spider-Man*.

One day, Emma may step out of the spotlight. She'd like to get behind the camera and produce her own films. For now, though, she's front and center, living the life of a movie star.

EMMA
PICS!

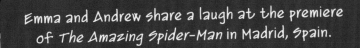

Emma and Andrew share a laugh at the premiere of *The Amazing Spider-Man* in Madrid, Spain.

SOURCE NOTE

7   "*Saturday Night Live* Clip (Emma Stone Monologue)," IMDb, clip from Hulu.com,
     televised by NBC on October 23. 2010, http://www.imdb.com/video/hulu
     /vi2584254745/.

MORE EMMA INFO

Emma Stone Biography
http://www.biography.com/people/emma-stone-20874773
Learn more about the star's life story.

Higgins, Nadia. *Logan Lerman: The Perks of Being an Action Star*. Minneapolis: Lerner
Publications, 2014. If you liked reading about Emma, you'll love this fun bio on Logan Lerman—
another up-and-coming star of the big screen.

IMDb Emma Stone
http://www.imdb.com/name/nm1297015
Get a complete list of Emma's acting credits.

People, Celebrity Central, Emma Stone Biography
http://www.people.com/people/emma_stone/biography
Travel through an Emma Stone timeline—with pics!

Us Weekly, "Emma Stone's Hair Evolution"
http://www.usmagazine.com/celebrity-beauty/pictures/emma-stones-hair-
evolution-2012211/25884
See how Emma's changed her hair color and style over the years.